365 IDEAS

To Go From Good To Great At NETWORKING!

John Sparks

365 Ideas To Go From Good To Great At NETWORKING!

First Printing 2016

ISBN-13: 978-1540480019
ISBN-10: 1540480011

Cover Design and Interior Format by James Subramanian
Cover Bio Picture by Stevie Cee at Studio Capturious

Praise for

365 Ideas To Go From Good To Great At NETWORKING!

"Networking is an essential skill, yet so many people struggle with it. This is a step by step guide to networking done right in today's day and age. Two huge Likeable thumbs up!"

—Dave Kerpen,
NY Times Bestselling Author of The Art of People

"John Sparks will light your social media on fire with this book."

—Jeffrey Hayzlett,
Primetime TV & Podcast Host,
Chairman C-Suite Network

"John has combined his own deep experience with that of other business networking gurus to bring you this invaluable guide. It's a quick read and worth exponentially more than the time you will invest in it. After reading 365 Ideas, please put the strategies into action!"

—Viveka von Rosen,
Forbes Top Ten Most Influential Women
on Social Media, Bestselling author
of LinkedIn Marketing: An Hour a Day, and 101 Ways
to Rock your Personal Brand with LinkedIn

"A network gives you reach, but a community gives you power! Networks connect . . . communities care. So follow John's advice on building your network . . . then create powerful communities."

—Ted Rubin,
author of Return on Relationship,
Keynote Speaker, Brand Evangelist, and
acting CMO of Brand Innovators

"John writes the book for the modern day networker! He shows how to use social media to turn online interactions into offline relationships. Must read!"

—Barry Moltz,
author, speaker, and radio show host
of Business Insanity Radio, AM560 WIND, Chicago

To those who enjoy networking, are looking for ideas to be better at networking, and are interested in infusing their entrepreneurial spirit here and around the world.

TABLE OF CONTENTS

INTRODUCTION

Who do you know? If you want to be successful and make money in business, the people you know and the relationships you maintain must be of the right quality.

People will buy what you are selling if they know you and like you. It does not always matter what the product or service is.

Since the people you know and how you present yourself in public are the identity of both you and your business, from my experience, here are 365 Ideas To Go From Good To Great At NETWORKING!

PART 1

What Networking Is and Why You Need to Be Good at It

 Idea #1: Understand What Networking Is and Is Not

Networking involves forming relationships with other people with the purpose of converting those relationships into business, and cultivating and retaining long-term contacts.

Networking:

- ▲ Involves developing long-lasting relationships with longer-term goals.
- ▲ Focuses on understanding others and their interests.
- ▲ Puts people before sales.

▲ Can lead to long lasting relationships which
   focus on service, retention, repeat purchases, and referrals.

Service, retention, repeat purchases, and referrals are
more likely to happen when people know, like, and trust
you. Know, like, and trust typically happens quicker in
one-on-one situations that take place offline. Therefore,
it is just as important (if not more important) to spend
time building a presence offline, as it is online.

 ## Idea #2: Understand the Easiest Way to Start Networking

Networking is easiest when you can see the people
with whom you are speaking. Both parties feel they are
relating to one another. Much of this relating is through
interpersonal communication.

▲ About 55% of a message we convey to
   others is through body language, while
   38% is by tone of voice.

▲ It is difficult to see body language or hear
   tone of voice in a tweet or Facebook post.

Where can you go to see, experience, and participate
in interpersonal communication with others? Find any
place where groups of people, get-togethers, or events
assemble and join in. It's always a great place to start!

Idea #3 Learn the Biggest Misconceptions About Networking

▲ Being good at networking means you have to be the organizer of events just to bring in potential leads and clients and to get new business.

▲ Being an attendee, who regularly visits business networking groups and events, carries just as much weight and can be just as valuable as being an organizer.

▲ The attendees are the ones who take time out of their schedule to show up, and time is the most important thing you can give someone.

Idea #4: Networking Is Important for Entrepreneurs but Why Is It Also Important in the Corporate World?

The business landscape continues to evolve and change. It does not matter which industry we are speaking of, as every industry has become extremely competitive.

▲ In today's competitive climate, what gives one business the advantage over the others?

✦   The business with the competitive advantage, that wins customers at the end of the day, is the company focused on networking and customer experience (CX).

Idea #5: Why Businesses Focused on Networking and Customer Experience Excel

▲   Companies focused on networking and customer experience (CX) have employees acting as "brand ambassadors."

▲   Brand ambassadors go out in public and serve as living examples of the core values, mission, and vision of the companies with which they work.

▲   As they focus on networking and customer experience, these brand ambassadors are the face of their company.

▲   It is important for those in this role to be out meeting others at networking events. They need to amplify the brand of the company they work for and bring in more prospects.

Idea #6: Networking Starts With Self-Awareness

▲ Good networking starts with self-awareness. Be aware of your gifts and talents before offering them to others.

▲ Know your personality, identify your expectations, and fearlessly examine both your strengths and your weaknesses.

▲ Consider taking an assessment to identify your talents like **Gallup's Clifton StrengthsFinder**, or a personality test like the **Myers-Briggs**.

 ## Idea #7: Understand Everyone Has Something to Offer Someone When Networking

What do you have to offer others that no one else has? You are uniquely and wonderfully made. There is not another person like you.

Exercise:

▲ Make a list of words that describe you.

▲ Ask others to write down a list of words that describe you.

▲ What similarities and differences do you find in these two lists?

The skills that distinguish you from everyone else are your core competencies.

Your core competencies make up the value that you can provide to others. You want to ensure others see this value when they meet you time and time again.

▲ Write out these core competencies on index cards and carry them around in a planner or pocketbook.

▲ Refer to the core competencies at least weekly.

▲ The list will help you maintain focus and direction during your journey.

▲ The list will serve as a guide in decision-making along the way.

 ### Idea #8: Understand How Networking Works and the Importance of Networking Events

▲ To have relationships with people, you have to meet people.

▲ There are two ways you can meet people: *online* or *offline*.

▲ Conversion rates are higher offline than online, and the goal should be to move relationships from online to offline.

This book provides ideas and tools to be successful in networking. It also helps you become familiar with online resources and apps that will bring you business.

Idea #9: "You Can Have Everything in Life You Want If You Will Just Help Enough Other People Get What They Want."

This insightful quote from Zig Ziglar is at the heart of networking. Said another way, *"People reach out to people who reach out."* The rewards are high for both parties if you're willing to help others achieve their goals.

Idea #10: Be Brave and Take Risks

To be successful at networking, you have to get your brave on and take risks!

Consider these questions:

- ▲ How much trust are you willing to put in someone you just met for the first time?
- ▲ What types of risks, and how many risks are you willing to take?
- ▲ Are you scared of failure?

To succeed at networking, you need to be willing to go somewhere you haven't gone before and try new things.

Idea #11: Understand We Are Designed for Community

▲ Use of the internet has caused us to move towards embracing more of an individualistic culture.

▲ With everyone online these days, the definition of togetherness and where we go to find it has shifted.

▲ We rely on our computer now more than ever to provide a sense of togetherness.

▲ We were designed with a purpose to participate in a larger community that doesn't always involve computers.

▲ Anyone who is making money and is succeeding in networking understands these realities.

 ## Idea #12: Beware: There Is Danger in Isolation

You have to get out there and shake hands with other people you haven't met before! Notice I said *shake hands*—not just send friend requests through Facebook, follow people on Twitter, or send them LinkedIn requests. You need to shake hands with other people *and* send them social media connection requests, but understand you might achieve more by meeting people in public.

Idea #13: Understand Networking Isn't Only about Having Relationships, It's about Having Deep Relationships with People

As you become better at networking and relationships deepen, so will your pocketbook, but it is important to keep focused on people.

Decide which people you enjoy being around most. Practice moving past cursory conversations with these individuals. Ask questions; listen. More in-depth conversations will bring you closer to people.

Be sure to feed and nourish relationships. Follow up and keep in touch with those whom you come into contact. Over time, the value of these relationships will increase significantly.

 Idea #14: Understand That the Focus of Networking Should Never Be You

Being in a relationship means "dying to yourself" daily. Disagreements will sometimes arise, and when they do, it's important to find out how to achieve a win-win. Ask yourself if the issue matters. "Winning" is never as important as the relationship.

Idea #15: Understand That Networking Isn't About Just Putting Yourself in a Position to Be Blessed, but to Bless Others

▲ Jot down the names of 5 people each day and find a way to be a blessing in their lives.

▲ Think of ways to compliment other people and make them feel good.

✦ Tell someone you like something they did.

✦ Deliver a meal to someone who has lost a loved one or is struggling with an illness.

✦ Find a non-profit and volunteer for a few hours each month.

▲ Whatever you choose to do, it is important to do this with no expectations in return.

✦ When there are no expectations in return, you are investing and sowing seeds into the lives of other people.

Idea #16:
Write Down Goals

▲ Set a timer for 10 minutes.

▲ Use index cards to write down goals to improve relationships and bless others.

▲ Put the index cards in a plastic zipper bag.

▲ Carry them around wherever you may go, and review them at least once or twice daily.

 ### Idea #17:
Keep a Daily Journal

▲ Keep a daily journal listing the accomplishments you've made towards reaching your relationship goals.

▲ Use the journal to brainstorm and plan out a "road map" to follow.

▲ Also use the journal as a tool to hold yourself accountable.

Idea #18: Understand the Key Differences Between an Accountability Partner and a Mentor

Mentoring is a support role. Sometimes a mentor can be an accountability partner, but not always.

▲ Accountability partners work *with* you.

▲ Mentors have gone *before* you.

 ## Idea #19: Get an Accountability Partner

It is easy to stay busy, but are you staying busy doing the right kinds of activities to build your business?

▲ Find someone you trust with whom you can check in on a weekly basis.

✦ This person must be willing to ask all those tough questions that others will bypass to avoid offending you or hurting your feelings.

✦ This person has to be someone with whom you can be honest.

✦ This person needs to be someone who is consistent, is willing to meet regularly, and has time to invest in you.

Idea #20: Work on Building Successful Accountability Partner Relationships

Work diligently to build strong accountability partner relationships. These strong relationships can help lead to a successful business. Accountability partner relationships are a two-way street.

▲ Meet with your accountability partner on a regular basis.

▲ Be transparent with your accountability partner. Share with each other things that are going well, in addition to areas of weakness with which you both struggle.

▲ Challenge one another, and hold each other accountable to anything discussed during the meetings.

▲ Understand change can take time. Do not try to overcome too many obstacles at once.

▲ Follow up with each other between meetings.

▲ Encourage one another.

Idea #21: Understand How to Find a Mentor

Most successful mentor/mentee relationships evolve over a length of time. When choosing a mentor, think about the people in your circle of influence who have spent time with you. Many times we already have mentors and do not even know we have them. Frequently, they are much closer than we realize.

 ## Idea #22: Work on Building Successful Mentor/Mentee Relationships

▲ Mentors should encourage mentees to develop their gifts and talents. These gifts should be separate from those of the mentor.

▲ Mentors should not try to change the mentee but instead help them grow. Mentors can help mentees understand their blind spots.

▲ Mentors must not assert domination over personal decision making.

▲ A successful mentor/mentee relationship will be relationship-based versus transactional-based. Establish good conversation criteria within the relationship.

▲ A mentoring relationship should have an end date.

▲ After the end date, it's important there is a flow of affirmation and appreciation between the mentor and the mentee.

 Idea #23: Know the Mistakes to Avoid in Mentor/Mentee Relationships

Avoid these common mistakes when embarking upon mentor/mentee relationships:

Mentor:

▲ Avoid picking a mentee who is not transparent or trustworthy.

▲ Avoid infrequent contact with your mentee. In other words, do not wait for your mentee to contact you. The mentee may think they are bothering you and hold back, so be intentional about making time for them.

▲ Avoid thinking that this is merely a one-way relationship. Mentors can and do learn from the mentee.

Mentee:

▲ Avoid picking a mentor who is not transparent or trustworthy.

▲ Avoid thinking the only person who can mentor you is someone with similar life experiences and perspectives. The goal of the relationship is for you to learn new things and to grow.

▲ Avoid the mindset that your mentor must be someone who looks just like you, shares the same background, or is your age.

▲ Avoid picking a mentor who suggests that they want to turn you into a duplicate of themselves.

▲ Avoid asking someone to be your mentor the first time you meet. Instead, thank the person for their time, and ask them if you can have a follow-up conversation with them in a couple of months.

 Idea #24:
Attend Networking Groups

Now that you have an accountability partner and a mentor, get out and meet new people! Make it a point to attend three networking groups each week. Attend networking groups both inside your industry and outside your industry.

Idea #25: Have a Plan Before Attending Networking Groups

Planning is crucial. Schedule networking events on your calendar that are at least one week after the RSVP date. If you're a first-time attendee, this will give you an opportunity to do research on the group before you go. You'll want to learn as much as you can about the group and its organizers. Knowing this information in advance could help determine if you still want to attend the group and invest your time.

Also, reflect on what you plan to accomplish when you attend a networking group. Part of having a plan means coming up with a business card and preparing a 30-second introduction ("elevator pitch").

Idea #26: Make Sure the Little Pieces Come Together Before Going to a Networking Event

Many small pieces must come together before attending a networking event. Items you might want to have when you go to an event include:

- ▲ Business cards
- ▲ Phone with a business card reader app
- ▲ Credit card reader (if you're selling products)

- ▲ Notepad or note taking app
- ▲ Mints or breath strips
- ▲ Water to stay hydrated
- ▲ Billfold/purse
- ▲ Handkerchiefs
- ▲ Pens/Writing Utensils

 ## Idea #27: Know How to Handle Difficult People

Acknowledge from the beginning that you cannot force other people to like you or act in a certain way. Put yourself in a position so that no matter how things turn out at a networking event, you have given 100%.

 ## Idea #28: Focus on Long-Term Results Instead of Short-Term Gains

Retaining customers over longer periods of time should be one of the goals of networking. It's more expensive to acquire a new customer than to retain one you already have.

Idea #29: Even Though Relationships Are Hard Work, Networking Should Look Like Something You Love to Do

Individuals and businesses, who are most successful at making money through networking, never make networking look like work because it's the driving force behind everything they do. Look around—these networkers don't just do it from 8 to 5. Networking keeps happening well after the work day is done.

PART 2

Clean up Your Own Backyard

 Idea #30:
Clean up Your Online Brand

Before trying to make an impact on others and help others, it's a good idea to have your online brand cleaned up:

1. *Submission to directories*: Send submissions to the top online directories to quickly build links to your website that search engines can see.

    ✦ These submissions to directories promote keywords and categorize your business.

2. *Keyword Link Building:* Build links on sites directly related to relevant vertical keywords.

    ✦ Link building provides credibility and trust for your business.

    ✦ Link building establishes your business as a leader in its industry.

    ✦ Link building can help diversify where links appear.

3. *Remove Toxic Links:* Toxic or harmful links need to be removed as best you can.

    ✦ Removing toxic links helps improve credibility, likeability, and SEO success.

In addition to taking these steps online, there are also steps you can take offline. The rest of Part 2 discusses more online and offline strategies to help you clean up your backyard.

 ## Idea #31: Get a Basic Presence on the Web

▲ Your #1 business is YOU.

▲ Companies, who are bought, sold and traded, go through name changes very quickly. However, your personal name will always be the same.

▲ Take control of your SEO by building
   citations to your personal name first.
   Afterward, build citations to your company
   name.

 ## Idea #32: Purchase Your Own Name as a Domain Name

How can you take control of your personal SEO if you
have not purchased your name as a website domain?

▲ You always want to own your personal
   name as a website domain.

▲ Be creative. If someone already has
   your name, come up with a spin-off or
   nickname.

   ✦ For example, purchase
      IAmYourName.com instead of
      YourName.com

▲ Do not wait! Purchase your personal name
   as a website domain name right now.

   ✦ There are plenty of places which sell
      domain names.

      • *GoDaddy, HostGator,* and *BlueHost*
         are three companies which offer
         domain registration services.

         ◇ See Appendix 1 for a listing of
            their website URLs.

> ✧ Google *"buy a website domain"* to find other companies who offer similar services.

Waiting to purchase a domain name is a classic mistake many people have made and continue to make when beginning their path to success. In fact, when the internet was starting out some of the top superstars of our time overlooked buying their personal name as a domain. Marketers would buy the names and sell them back for thousands of dollars. If you don't have the money to buy your domain name back, don't make the same mistake.

Idea #33: Use <u>Namechk.com</u> to Help Pick Domain Names, Vanity URLs, and Usernames

Namechk.com tells users if a domain name is available. It also tells you if a name is available as a vanity social media URL and username.

- ▲ Choose a name that's available as both a domain name, vanity social media URL, and username on all the main social media sites.

  - ✦ The name should be available as a dot-com, but should also be available for use on Facebook, Twitter, LinkedIn, Instagram, Pinterest, YouTube, and Google+.

Note: Namechk.com may indicate a name is in use when
it isn't (and vice versa). It's always best to go through the
process of double-checking *ALL* URLs and usernames,
on the social media sites themselves, before changing
any of them or spending money to commit to a new
domain name.

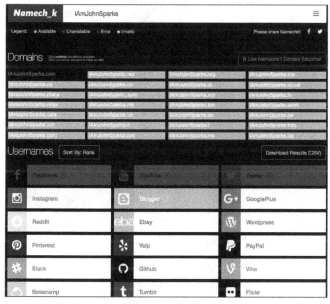

Screenshot 2-1

*Use Namechk.com for branding: to pick domain names, social
media URLs, and usernames.*

Idea #34:
Purchase a DBA

Register and purchase a DBA *(Doing Business As)* with the local and county government. Use <u>Namechk.com</u> to ensure domain names, social media URLs, and user-names are available before purchasing a DBA.

Idea #35: Buy Your Business Name as a Domain Name Immediately after You Register the DBA

▲ It is fine to sign up and register for vanity social media URLs and usernames before purchasing a DBA.

▲ Wait to purchase domain names until after registering the name with the local and county government.

✦ Do this to avoid spending any unnecessary money.

Act quickly! Purchase the domain name from your mobile device immediately after registering your DBA.

Do not wait! Remember, savvy marketers who have access to new filings might try to register and purchase the domain name before you do. These marketers will try to resell it back to you for thousands of dollars!

Idea #36:
Get a PO Box for Your Business

A PO box helps protect the privacy of your business, especially if you have a small business and are working from home. Do not feel obliged to give someone your home address. In some cases, delivery to a PO box can mean quicker mail service than home delivery, especially if a PO box is inside the U.S. Post Office.

Idea #37: Understand How to
Register a PO Box Online

Local search engine websites won't allow you to use a PO box as a business address. There is a workaround:

- ▲ Find out the physical street address of the post office or mailbox center where your PO box is.
- ▲ Enter the physical address on the online forms as the street address.
- ▲ Enter your box number as the apartment number or suite number.

Idea #38: Get a Virtual Business Address for Your Business

If you're concerned about people looking up your business address and checking to see if it's truly an office then get a virtual office:

- ▲ When others search the address of a virtual office, they'll get a listing and see a picture of a professional office building.

- ▲ With a virtual office, you don't have to be concerned if someone tries to stop by, or tries to drop something off for you.

   - ✦ Many virtual offices have receptionists that greet visitors.

- ▲ With a virtual office, you get the benefit of sharing a staff that to some extent works for you and represents your company.

 ## Idea #39: Understand the Role Search Engines Play in Cleaning up Your Backyard

With the changes search engines continue to make, getting found on the first page of results is no easy task. In fact, it keeps getting more and more difficult.

While there are things you can try to do to get your name on the first page of results, there are no guarantees.

- ▲ The internet is an increasingly complicated environment.

- ▲ Algorithms are forever changing, and changing rapidly.

At the end of the day, the choice becomes yours: you can choose to do nothing, do it yourself, or hire someone to help you do it.

Why pay to play, especially if there are no guarantees? Do the best you can to follow the ideas below to optimize for local search listings.

Budget 2–3 hours to find all the sites, open accounts, and update listings with the most current information.

Idea #40: Optimize Your Business on Local Search Listings

So others can find your business, make sure the local search listings have the most up-to-date information on you and your business.

Optimizing submissions to local search listings will quickly build links that search engines can see that promote keywords and also categorize your business.

Every directory you appear in is another opportunity for others to see you online. Therefore, make sure you're listed in every directory possible.

Idea #41: Understand How to Navigate Local Search Sites

Optimizing and listing yourself and your business on local search listings can take time.

▲ Many of these websites are complex and challenging to navigate.

▲ The websites continuously change their URLs and the process for signing up.

▲ Many articles and blog posts written on this topic won't direct you to the local search websites. Instead, they'll link you to a third-party company where you'll be asked to pay to sign up.

Idea #42: Know the Top 10 Business Directory Sites to Have Your Business Listed

Source: Top 10 Free USA Local Business Directory Sites List 2016-2017

1. Google Local Places
2. Yelp for Business Owners
3. Bing Places for Business
4. Merchant Circle

5. Local.com

6. Expressupdate.com

7. Yext and MapQuest

8. Insiderpages.com

9. Foursquare for Business

10. Abaco Small Business from Yahoo
    (Formerly Yahoo Small Business)

Screenshot 2-2

Adding and updating a listing to Yext and MapQuest.

Idea #43: Know How to Add Your Business Name to the Top 10 Business Directory Sites

Make sure to both create an account *AND* add a listing for your business on each of the local search websites.

- ▲ Opening an account is *NOT* the same as adding a listing. It's a different process.
    - ✦ First, create an account.
    - ✦ Next, "add a listing."
- ▲ Links to "add a listing" can usually be found at the very top of a site or at the very bottom.

Idea #44: Know Where to Find Listings of More Business Directory Sites

Learn the names of the local business directories that are worth signing up for. There are several lists of business directories. Site rankings will differ depending on the list.

Here are the website links to several listings of local business directories:

- ▲ "Top 10 Free USA Local Business Directory Sites List 2016-2017"

  http://www.ads2020.marketing/2014/02/10-free-usa-local-business-sites-2014.html

- ▲ "Top 20 Local Business Directories You Need To Be On"

  http://localvox.com/blog/top-local-business-directories/

- ▲ "The Ultimate List: 50 Online Local Business Directories"

  http://blog.hubspot.com/blog/tabid/6307/bid/10322/The-Ultimate-List-50-Local-Business-Directories.aspx-sm.000018xkhd737ne1xvwdopuoq5qhi

- ▲ "Top 15 Local Directory Listing Services"

  http://www.practicalecommerce.com/articles/115895-top-15-local-directory-listing-services

- ▲ "Top 50 Local Citation Sites – US, UK, Canada And Australia"

  https://www.brightlocal.com/2013/09/11/top-50-local-citation-sites/

Screenshot 2-3

The Ultimate List: 50 Online Local Business Directories.

Again, be cautious, as some of the hyperlinks found on these listings may not take you to the correct business directory sites to register. If this happens, just Google the business directory site that you are looking for.

Idea #45:
Be Ready for the Phone to Ring

Once you start adding your name to the business directory listings, be ready for the phone to ring. The people calling at first probably won't be the new business you're hoping for. Instead, it'll most likely be telemarketers trying to up-sell you into purchasing better listings with their companies. Be smart—just say no.

 ## Idea #46:
Make Friends with the Past

Quoting Zig Ziglar: "You are at the top when you have made friends with the past …"

▲ Reflect, address, and heal past issues. If needed, cut ties with things others might find offensive.

▲ Remember the rule of six degrees of separation. You never know how people are connected, and how some of these people might be able to lend a voice to what you're doing.

▲ When you are friends with the past, you can focus more on the present. It's also easier to be optimistic about the future!

PART 3
Business Cards 101

 Idea #47: Design Your Business Card to Gain Trust

▲ A business card is an essential tool for becoming successful in networking.

▲ Some allow their creative juices to run wild when they create their business cards and don't need to.

▲ Keep your business card simple, but make a statement with it.

Idea #48: Model Your Card after the Best in the Business

▲ Some of the best business cards are those belonging to realtors and financial advisors.

▲ Realtors and financial advisors realize they are in personality-driven professions where relationships of trust are paramount. As a result, most realtors and financial advisors have their picture on their business card.

▲ Realtors and financial advisors are in a profession where competition is steep. They realize they only have one chance to make a lasting impression. As a result, their business cards also have great branding and messaging.

Idea #49: Put Your Picture on Your Business Card

When connecting with your audience, putting a picture of yourself on your card will help you achieve several things:

1. Having a photograph (headshot) of yourself is a way to show your personality and customize your card.

✦   No one else will have the same picture
on their card; no one looks like you.

2.   It will help others find you easier when
they get home and start connecting online.

✦   Since people you meet might forget
what you look like, having a picture
on your card will help others decide
if they're connecting with the right
person online (especially if you have a
common name).

 ### Idea #50: Use the Same Picture on Your Business Cards That You Use on Your Social Media Sites

People won't work hard to find you online; they just won't. When the picture on your business card matches the one on your online profiles, others will be reassured that they are connecting with you.

 ### Idea #51: Know How and Where to Put Your Picture on Your Card

▲   Size: Make sure the photo takes up 1/4 of
the card.

▲   Location: Put the photo on the left side of
the card. People read from left to right. You
want them to see your picture first.

▲ Use of space: Make sure the picture stretches from the very top of the card to the very bottom.

Idea #52: Have Your Picture Taken by a Professional Photographer

▲ Have a professional photographer take your picture for your business card.

▲ You want someone to take your picture who has experience with lighting, exposure, highlights, shadows, brightness, contrast, definition, color, backgrounds, and white balance.

▲ This expenditure will pay for itself many times over.

Idea #53: Don't Forget the Makeup

▲ Don't forget to touch up any blemishes and unwanted redness on your face before getting your pictures taken.

▲ Stop by the makeup counter at any department store. Most makeup professionals will give you a free makeover right before your photographs are taken.

▲ Most makeup artists at department stores will use the best makeup they have, and catch areas you might miss if you decide to put the makeup on yourself.

 ## Idea #54: Make Sure Your Card Is Legible and Easy to Read

▲ Some people try using different fonts to make their name and other parts of their business card stand out. They may use a font to attract people's attention.

▲ Some cursive fonts and special fonts are hard to read. Vowels can be difficult to read. For example, the letter "a" may look similar to the letter "o."

▲ Avoid using cursive fonts and special fonts on your card. Don't risk someone having to guess the spelling of your name when they try to search for you on LinkedIn, or another social media platform.

▲ Think about the fonts you decide to use on your card. Use either an Arial, Helvetica, or Times New Roman font.

Idea #55: Understand Why Your Name Should Be on the Second Line Instead of the First Line of Your Business Card

1. List your name on the second line of your business card. Put the name of your company or a professional headline before your name, on the first line of your business card.

2. Many people who go to networking groups use business card scanners (CamCard, or similar apps) to add data from business cards to their contact list on their phones.

3. If your name appears on the first line of your card, business card scanners will list your name in the company field, instead of the name field, of a contact listing.

4. The person scanning your card will have to go back and edit your contact data. Again, you want to make it as easy as possible on those who you're giving your information to. They'll be thankful you've saved them the time.

Idea #56: Understand Why You May Not Need a Business Logo on Your Card

Business logos take up real estate on your card and cost money to make.

▲ Does every business card need a logo? *The answer is "No."*

▲ Since people prefer to do business with people they know, like, and trust, having a picture of *you* on the card could be a better use of space than having a logo. (Remember, a picture will also help others find you quicker when they are connecting online).

▲ When deciding to use a logo, consider these questions:

✦ Does your business already have a brand logo people associate with it?
✦ What is the size of the company?
✦ What is your industry?
✦ What are others doing who are in your same industry?

▲ People who work for small businesses, people who work for companies that don't have a brand logo others already identify with, and people who are in personality driven industries are typically better off with a picture of themselves on their card, instead of a logo.

Idea #57: Use a White Background on Your Business Card

▲ Use a white background on your business cards.

▲ Black cards and color cards are harder to read and scan.

▲ Often times others have to manually enter data found on black or color cards.

▲ Using a white background is a way to stand out and show you're a networker who knows what they're doing.

 ## Idea #58: Use a Matte Finish for Your Business Card

Several people who attend networking groups will want to jot down notes on your business card. Some will want to write on the front. Others will want to write on the back.

▲ Cards with a matte finish will allow writing on either side.

▲ Cards with a matte finish are easy to scan. Cards with a glossy finish are hard to scan.

▲ A cell phone flash will cause reflected light to leave a big, white spot covering up information on cards with a glossy finish.

Idea #59: Make Sure the Card's Message Makes Sense

When you exchange cards, you won't have a chance to explain why it looks the way it does. You'll just give the card to the person and the recipient will interpret it later. Therefore, be sure that both the card and its message makes sense. Also, remember humor may not translate well.

Idea #60: Keep the Content on Your Business Card Simple

Don't try to squeeze too much information onto your business card.

Include the following information on your card:

▲ What you do

▲ Your name

▲ Cell phone number

▲ A single email address

▲ One website URL

▲ Where others can find you on the big three social media sites (Facebook, Twitter, and LinkedIn).

Leave everything else off your card. Less is more.

Idea #61: Choose the Best Phone Numbers to Put on Your Business Card

Make it easy for others to contact you when they need you.

▲ When others receive your card, they shouldn't have to spend time deciphering the best phone number to enter into their contact list to reach you.

▲ The first phone number listed on your card should be a number you want others to try and call you at first. The phone number shouldn't always go to voice mail.

▲ Don't put useless contact information on your business card (e.g. an office phone number when you're never in the office). Use the real estate on your card for more important things.

 ## Idea #62: Consider Removing the Fax Number from Your Business Card

▲ Consider removing the fax number from your business card.

▲ Wait until others ask for your fax number, and then write the number for them on your card. In the meantime, use the space on your card for something more important.

Idea #63: Know Which Social Media Links to Include on Your Business Card

▲ Include the social media links for Facebook, Twitter, and LinkedIn on your business card (assuming you are active on all three of these social media sites, which you should be!).

▲ If you have an account on one of these sites but aren't active on it, then don't include it on your card.

  ✦ You don't want to risk someone trying to contact you on a site where you rarely check your activity, messages, and notifications.

  ✦ You don't want someone going to one of these sites and wondering if you know what you're doing or if you're going to reply.

Idea #64: Ask Other Networkers What They Think of Your Business Card before You Pay to Have Them Printed

▲ You might think you have a great concept for a business card, but it needs to be functional too.

▲ Ask others in your network to give you feedback on your card before you spend money printing it.

   ✦ Does the business card make sense?

   ✦ Is the card a good reflection of you, your brand, and your personality?

   ✦ Does the card have good messaging?

   ✦ Do others like the picture on your card?

   ✦ Does the card get the job done?

Idea #65: Pick a Printer That Makes "Cents"

There are many great local printers and designers out there who can help you print your cards. Some of these people are at some of the networking events and Meetup groups. There are also online options available. Ask around. Pick a printer that saves time, money, and offers a quality product.

Idea #66: Find Someone Who Will Design and Print Your Business Cards for the Price of One

You can get both a printer and designer, for the price of one, by using sites like Vistaprint. Currently you can:

▲ Set up an account on Vistaprint's website.

▲ Put together a rough draft of your business card with Vistaprint's online design tool.

▲ Call Vistaprint customer service. Tell a customer service rep that you need help designing and laying out your card.

▲ Vistaprint agents will help you clean up the rough draft of your business card. Most of the agents are also willing to help design your card for you. Just tell them how you want your finished card to look.

▲ The best part about Vistaprint is that they only charge for the printing.

 ## Idea #67: Print Your Business Cards on Signature Card Stock

When you print your card, be sure to use signature card stock. A signature stock is heavier than the standard stock. It's also super durable and has a more professional look.

 ## Idea #68: Ask for a Discount on Your Business Cards

Ask for a discount from whoever you use to print your cards. Many times you can get up to 50% off the prices advertised online. Shop and compare, but don't forget to ask if there's a way to save even more money!

Idea #69: Keep Business Cards with You at All Times

Look at your business cards like money. Don't leave home without them. Keep them on you at all times. You never know who you're going to run into. Networking can happen anywhere—even on a simple trip to the grocery store. Be prepared!

Idea #70: Don't Be a Card Pusher

Your business card is one of the most powerful tools in networking. Don't give it out too soon.

▲   Don't fall into the trap of attending events where people are freely handing out their business cards and feel like you should be doing the same.

▲   Have a conversation with someone at an event before giving out your personal information.

▲   Wait until someone asks you for your card first.

Idea #71: Be Aware of Information Gatherers and Card Collectors

There are a group of people who attend networking events just to gather contact information to build up their email lists.

At some point, you will encounter at least one person who fits into this category.

The fact that others are supposed to ask you for permission before adding your name to their email list won't necessarily stop them from going ahead and doing it.

 Idea #72: What You Should Do If Someone from a Networking Event Adds You to Their Email Subscription List

This is spamming. You didn't request to be on their list.

▲ Unsubscribe to their list.

▲ Contact the individual by phone, or talk to them in person. Be direct and express your concerns with them.

▲ Contact the group organizer and let them know.

Idea #73: Download a Business Card Scanner Such as the CamCard App to Your Phone

Get rid of that stack of business cards you have. Business card scanners, like the CamCard app, quickly scan cards (in most cases automatically) and then add them to the contact list on your cell phone.

Screenshot 3-1

CamCard app in the Apple iTunes Store.

▲ **iPhone users can download the CamCard app by going to:**

https://itunes.apple.com/us/app/camcard -free-business-card/id355472887?mt=8

▲ Android users can download the CamCard app by going to:

https://play.google.com/store/apps/
details?id=com.intsig.BCRLite&hl=en

CamCard sorts business cards by the date the card was scanned into the app. If you scan the card right when you meet the person, you'll always know the day you met the person. CamCard also allows you to create a virtual card you can exchange with others, plus creates a QR Code that others (using the same app) can use to scan and import your information right into their app.

Screenshot 3-2

Business cards in CamCard appear by the date they are added.

There is a CamCard app which costs 99 cents, and there is also a free version. The free version should be sufficient for your needs when you're starting out.

 ## Idea #74: Set up Groups for Your Business Cards in CamCard

▲ Groups will assist you in locating the people you're looking for quickly when you need them.

▲ Create names of groups based on the location where you meet people.

▲ As you start connecting with more and more people, build relationships, and get to know others in one-to-ones, add more groups.

▲ The ultimate goal is to have more and more groups while reducing the number of people you have in each group.

▲ Eventually you'll get to know people so well that you won't need to look them up in a group, but instead can easily find them by first and last name. When you're looking for a certain business professional, they'll be the first person who comes to mind.

Screenshot 3-3

Groups in the CamCard app.

 ## Idea #75: Spend 30 Minutes per Day Updating CamCard

It'll take you some time to import all your business cards into the CamCard app, so have a plan.

▲ Spend 30 minutes per day:

✦ Importing new cards into the app on the same day you receive them, in addition to a handful of the old cards from your stash.

+ Once cards are imported, take time to make sure the cards scanned correctly.

+ Edit any fields where names, addresses, email addresses, and phone numbers fail to appear correctly.

+ Once you've imported the information from the cards into the app, you can shred the cards.

+ Create categories in CamCard and move the scanned cards to the appropriate categories.

 Idea #76: Know How to Share Contact Information (without a Business Card) Using the CamCard App

1. Select *"Profile"* (bottom menu bar in the CamCard app).

2. Select *"Send My Card."*

3. A pop-up menu will appear at the bottom of the screen.

4. Send your contact info by:

   + Email

   + SMS (text message)

   + Selecting "*QR Code*" to generate a QR Code that other users can scan

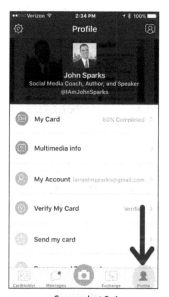

Screenshot 3-4

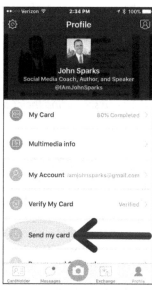

Screenshot 3-5

Screenshot 3-6

Screenshot 3-7

To share your contact information using the CamCard app, make sure that "Profile" is selected (bottom menu bar; Screenshot 3-4). Next, select "Send my Card" (Screenshot 3-5). When the pop-up menu appears, choose to send your contact information via email, SMS (text message), or QR Code (Screenshot 3-6). If selecting "QR Code," CamCard will generate a QR Code that others can scan using their CamCard app (Screenshot 3-7).

Idea #77: Know How to Share Contact Information (without a Business Card) Using Your iPhone Contact List

1. Create a contact listing for yourself in your iPhone.

2. Do a search for your name in your iPhone contact list.

3. Select your contact card to see the contact details.

4. Scroll to the bottom of your contact and select *"Share Contact."*

5. Share your vCard via email, SMS (text message), or another method you select.

Screenshot 3-8

Screenshot 3-9

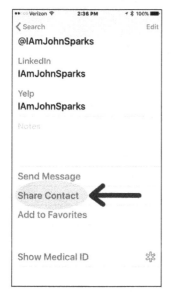

Screenshot 3-10

Screenshot 3-11

To share your contact information using the iPhone contact list, create a contact for yourself in your iPhone contact list (Screenshot 3-8). Do a search for your name (Screenshot 3-9), and retrieve your contact information. Scroll to the bottom of your contact information, and select "Share Contact" (Screenshot 3-10). Next, share your vCard via email, SMS (text message), or another method you select (Screenshot 3-11).

Idea #78: Know How to Share Contact Information without a Business Card Using Android Beam on a Samsung Galaxy

You can send your contact information wirelessly from one Samsung Galaxy to another, using near-field communication (NFC) and Android Beam.

▲ Locate your personal contact information on your phone or the contact information you want to share.

▲ Touch the phones together, back-to-back.

▲ To share the contact, the sender can touch anywhere on their screen.

▲ Once the contact is sent, the receiver will need to acknowledge receipt.

Idea #79: Be Familiar with Other Business Card Scanner Apps

Looking for other apps to help you digitize your cards? Here's a list of some popular business card scanner apps for iPhone and Android:

▲ **iPhone Business Card Scanner Apps**

> http://www.igeeksblog.com/best-business
> -card-reader-scanner-apps-for-iphone/

▲ **Android Business Card Scanner Apps**

> http://www.androidheadlines.
> com/2015/01/featured-top-10-business
> -card-scanner-apps-android.html

▲ **More iPhone and Android Business Card Scanner Apps**

> http://www.scrubly.com/blog/tech-tips/
> 5-great-business-card-apps-smartphone/

PART 4

Giving a Great 30-Second Introduction Offline

 Idea #80: Why You Need a 30-Second Introduction

One of the first things you'll do at a networking group is what's called the 30-second introduction. Attendees at a networking group go around the room and introduce themselves. Each person will have 30-seconds to make a powerful impression that can create buzz and get you noticed.

Idea #81: What Is the Purpose of Your 30-Second Introduction

Is the purpose of your 30-second introduction to:

a. Get more clients?

b. Get more business leads?

c. Get more networking opportunities?

d. Meet new people?

e. All of the above?

Knowing these answers in advance will help you determine what you should say during your 30-second introduction.

Idea #82: What Makes a Successful 30-Second Introduction

Here are some questions your 30-second introduction should help answer:

▲ Who are you?

▲ What do you do?

▲ Who are you looking to meet?

▲ Who are you looking to help?

▲ What types of problems have you solved?

- ▲ What are some of the accomplishments you've achieved?

- ▲ How can people in the networking group help you?

- ▲ What is a good referral or introduction for you?

 Idea #83: Your Introduction Is 30 Seconds, but You Only Have a Tenth of a Second to Hook Your Audience

In 2012, Jeffrey Hayzlett redefined what we know as the elevator pitch. Hayzlett calls the Elevator Pitch 2.0 digital version: *"The 118."*

- ▲ Hayzlett says, *"The 118"* breaks down into 8 seconds to hook your audience (the average attention span of an adult) and 110 seconds to close them (the length of a typical elevator ride in New York City).

Since most networking groups only give you 30 seconds to introduce yourself, you only have about a tenth of a second to make a memorable Impression. The extra 29.9 seconds is used to boost the confidence of others in any judgments they've already made.

Idea #84:
It Starts with Who You Are

At the very beginning, say your name. Your name is the most important part of your 30-second introduction.

▲ *First tell people who you are; then tell them what you do.*

I've seen many introductions where people are so preoccupied thinking about what they're about to say that they neglect to say their name at the beginning! Instead of focusing on what's being said, others listening focus on what should have been said. That's a wasted 30 seconds.

Idea #85:
Learn How to Say Your Name

▲ When speaking your name, create a strong vocal executive presence.

▲ Bring your intonation pattern and tone up on your first name, then bring the intonation pattern and tone down on the last name.

▲ At the beginning of your speech, pause between your first name and last name.

Watch this informative TEDx Talk by Vocal Impact Specialist, Dr. Laura Sicola, on how to say your name with confidence: http://bit.ly/SayUrName

Idea #86: Speak Loud and Clear

- ▲ Speak loud and clear during your 30-second introduction.
- ▲ Project your voice so others can hear you.
- ▲ This helps to create your own unique and authentic "sound of leadership."

Idea #87: Decide What You Offer and Identify Those You Are Looking to Connect with

After you say your name, then be sure to state:

1. What you are offering
2. Whom you'd like to connect with

This is called your value proposition. After your name, it's the second most important part of your 30-second introduction.

Idea #88: Use the Pregnant Pause to Overcome Distractions during Your Introduction

▲ Be prepared for people listening to your 30-second introduction to become distracted while you're talking.

▲ When distractions occur, pause and then repeat what you were saying over again. This way you make sure your message reaches the entire audience.

Idea #89: Repeat Your Name at the End of Your Introduction

During your introduction, people are taking in a lot of information during a short period of time. When you start talking about what you do, it's natural for some people to forget what you said at the beginning of your introduction—your name! Therefore, be sure to repeat your name again at the very end of your introduction.

Idea #90: Position Yourself in a Place Where You're Facing Everyone and Everyone Can See You

When you give your introduction, position yourself where you don't have your back to anyone.

▲ Move to the front or back of the room.

▲ If you're sitting down, stand up and move away from your chair.

▲ Remember, you want everyone to see you and hear you.

Idea #91: Practice Your Introduction, but Do Not Over-Practice

▲ Practice your introduction, but don't over-practice.

▲ If you practice it too much, your introduction won't sound natural.

+ Your introduction will sound memorized and rehearsed.

+ It will lack passion and energy.

+ Your natural enthusiasm won't come across. (It's important the audience has a chance to see this part of your personality).

Idea #92:
Be Spontaneous

One of the best introductions I've seen at a networking group was an improv. One of the members burst out into song and had another member join in. They were both having so much fun, they didn't care how badly they were embarrassing themselves. The room came alive, and people loved it! Afterward, everyone was buzzing about what they did, and it was a subject of discussion in all the post-event conversations. By being spontaneous and unscripted, they accomplished exactly what they set out to do: create an impression and make a statement that got people talking.

Idea #93:
Strive for the Memorable Moments

- ▲ Every 30-second introduction should have at least one memorable moment.

- ▲ A memorable moment is something unexpected that catches the audience by surprise.

Another memorable introduction I've seen at a networking group was a ventriloquist who brought along her sidekick "dummy." Her call to action, at the end of her introduction was: "Don't be a *dummy*—contact me for an insurance quote today!" Everyone remembered her 30-second introduction and was talking about it afterward.

Idea #94: Have Others Interact with You during Your 30-Second Introduction

▲ Take advantage of any opportunities you can to have others in your networking group interact with you during your 30-second introduction.

▲ Remember: "Speeches that grab and keep attention, stimulate agreement, and generate the speaker's desired results happen only when the presenter mixes action with interaction," said Dr. Bill Lampton, Speech, and C-Suite communication consultant.

Idea #95: Remember CLARITY Is Crucial

In his book, "The New Elevator Pitch", National Elevator Pitch Champion Chris Westfall said your speech must be clear to create the outcomes you want through effective storytelling and communication. Your speech should:

1. Have authenticity

2. Be compelling

3. Make others want to say: "*Tell me more.*"

Idea #96:
Practice Good Eye Contact

When talking to people, strike a balance between having too much eye contact and not enough eye contact.

- ▲ When talking to just one person:
    - ✦ Pick a point to focus on (eyes, forehead, nose, cheeks, chin, etc.).
    - ✦ Rotate your point of focus so you're not just staring at one place.

- ▲ When talking to multiple people in a room:
    - ✦ Don't keep your eyes focused on the same people.
    - ✦ Look at someone new approximately every 4 seconds.
    - ✦ In between breaking eye contact with one person and establishing it with someone new, don't look down. Look to the side instead.

Idea #97: SMILE during Your 30-Second Introduction

It's amazing how many resources say nothing about smiling during your 30-second introduction.

- ▲ "People judge smiling faces as trustworthy, and angry-looking faces as untrustworthy,"

said Dr. Peter Mende-Siedlecki,
a postdoctoral researcher in the NYU
psychology department.

▲ Pay attention to both your facial
  expressions and the non-verbal cues you
  are giving off.

▲ Pick up on the facial expressions and
  non-verbal cues you receive from your
  audience, and use them to adjust your
  facial expressions and non-verbal cues
  accordingly.

PART 5

Get in the Networking Game with Meetup

 Idea #98: Understand That the Only Game in Town Is Not Facebook, Twitter, and LinkedIn

While having a presence both online and offline is important, the relationships you build offline will deliver the highest conversion rate.

- ▲ Your online presence should be used to build these offline relationships.

- ▲ There are quite a few websites and apps available online to help you locate offline opportunities for building relationships and growing your business.

▲ To become a super connector, add several other websites to your toolbox in addition to Facebook, Twitter, and LinkedIn.

 **Idea #99:
Know What "Meetup" Is**

Meetup is a social networking site that helps its users find groups of other people online, who share the same interests and want to get together to meet offline.

You name it, and there's a Meetup Group for just about anything you can think of:

▲ Professional networking groups and careers

▲ Sports groups (hiking, walking, running clubs, etc.)

▲ Photography

▲ Gardening

▲ Singles groups

▲ Religious groups

▲ Parenting

▲ Moms' playgroups

Idea #100:
Know Where to Find Meetup

There are several ways you can find Meetup:

▲ **Meetup is available on the web at:**

http://www.Meetup.com

▲ **iPhone users can download the Meetup app by going to:**

https://itunes.apple.com/us/app/Meetup
-groups-near-you-that/id375990038?mt=8

▲ **Android users can download the Meetup app by going to:**

https://play.google.com/store/apps/
details?id=com.meetup&hl=en

Screenshot 5-1

Meetup app in the Apple iTunes Store.

 Idea #101: Understand the Ups and Downs of Meetup

Ups:

▲ There are many groups on Meetup.

✦ Over 240,000 different Meetup Groups are on <u>Meetup.com</u> according to the Meetup Blog.

▲ It's easy to get plugged into a Meetup Group.

✦ By default, you'll receive all emails from the groups that you join. Emails will include everything from a new Meetup that is scheduled to organizers posting announcements about a particular Meetup.

Downs:

▲ It can be confusing to decipher between a Meetup group page and a Meetup event page.

✦ Some of this confusion might appear to be intentional.

▲ The types of Meetup groups you will find in each city will vary.

✦ Some cities will offer a combination of both professional networking groups and casual get-togethers. Other cities will offer one and not the other.

▲ Changing your email preferences can be a challenging process.

▲ Using the "Messages" function can be a bit tricky.

✦ There's one way to contact the head organizer of a group and another way to contact designated multiple organizers of a group.

✦ The message form itself can be confusing. If not careful, it's easy to send a message to multiple organizers of a group instead of sending it to just one user.

✦ Generally speaking, the return response rate on messages from others is quite low. Don't be surprised if you try to message someone on Meetup and don't get a response.

 ## Idea #102: Understand the Difference Between Meetup Groups And Meetups

▲ **Meetup Groups** are the groups themselves.

✦ Meetup Groups don't necessarily have to have any Meetup events listed.

✦ Meetup Group pages and Meetup event pages look very similar.

• <u>Meetup.com</u> makes money based on how big the groups are. One way Meetup groups grow is by having more Meetup events. (Therefore, don't be surprised if you have a hard time telling the difference between the event pages and the group pages.)

▲ **Meetups** are the events that are held by a
   particular group.

   ✦ Meetups can be online or offline.

   ✦ To post a Meetup on Meetup.com, the
      organizers must first create a group for
      the event or series of events.

   ✦ Meetups might have the same name as
      the group's name or a different name.

 **Idea #103: Bring Your Pocketbook
with You to Meetups**

▲ Make sure you bring extra cash with you
   when you attend a Meetup.

▲ While Meetup groups are supposed to
   post event fees on their event pages, some
   groups don't list them.

▲ Most organizers don't accept payments
   through Meetup.com because the website
   processing fees are high.

Idea #104: Know How to Search for New Meetup Groups

There are two ways to search for a new Meetup group using the web-based version:

1. Click the "Groups" tab on the homepage.

2. Click "Find a Meetup Group" at the top of any page.

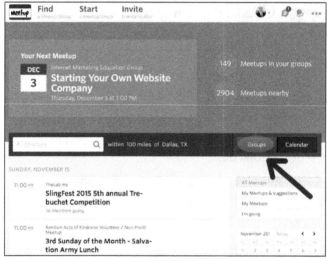

Screenshot 5-2

Screenshot 5-3

To search for new groups, click the "Groups" tab on the homepage (Screenshot 5-2) or click "Find a Meetup Group" at the top of any page on Meetup.com (Screenshot 5-3).

 ## Idea #105: Know How to Use The "Groups" Page to Locate Groups You Are Already In

▲ On the "Groups" page, under the section heading, "Your Meetups," you'll find a listing and links to the group pages of the groups you've already joined.

▲ Under "Your Meetups," you'll find "Suggested Meetups." These are groups you're not yet a member of but can join.

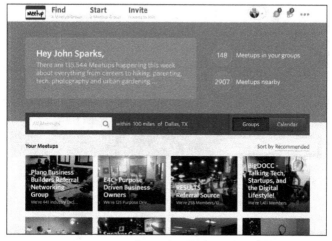

Screenshot 5-4

On the "Groups" page, under the section heading: "Your Meetups," you'll find a listing and links to the group pages of the groups you've already joined on Meetup.com

 ## Idea #106: Understand How The "Groups" Page Sorts Groups

▲ Groups listed on the "Groups" page on the web-based version of Meetup.com are sorted by default in "Recommended View."

✦ Groups that have Meetups happening the soonest appear first in ascending order.

✦ Groups with scheduled Meetups appear before groups with no scheduled Meetups.

Idea #107: Understand How You Can Use The "Groups" Page to Sort Groups

▲ In addition to the "Recommended View," there are four other ways to sort groups on the "Groups" page.

✦ Click *"Sort by Recommended"* (right side of the page).

✦ From here, groups can be sorted by "Most active," "Newest," "Most Members," and "Closest."

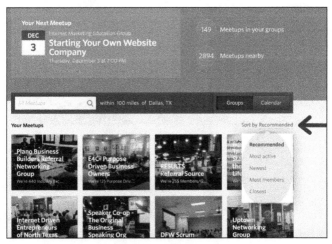

Screenshot 5-5

Sorting groups by "Recommended," "Most active," "Newest," "Most Members," and "Closest" on <u>*Meetup.com*</u>

Idea #108: Search for New Groups to Join on The "Groups" Page

There are several ways to search for new groups to join on the "Groups" page.

▲ Search the groups your friends are also attending.

▲ Search groups by suggested categories.

▲ Search groups by doing a keyword search.

Before joining a group, check out the group's page to find out if they have any Meetups scheduled.

Screenshot 5-6

Searching for new groups on Meetup.com

Idea #109: Know How to Search for New Groups by Location on The "Groups" Page

▲ Search for the groups closest to you on the "Groups" page.

✦ Adjust distance settings to the right of the Meetup search bar on the homepage.

✦ Locate groups within a certain mile radius of a city or Zip Code of your choice.

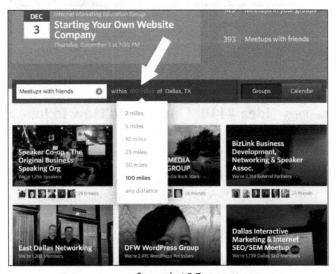

Screenshot 5-7

Locating groups by mile radius on Meetup.com

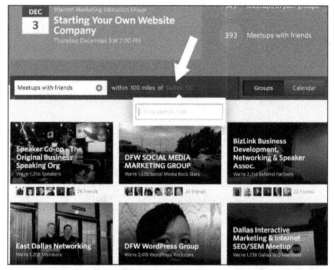

Screenshot 5-8

Locate groups in a city or ZIP Code on <u>Meetup.com</u>

Idea #110: Understand How to Join a Group on Meetup

▲ To join a group on <u>Meetup.com</u>, click the *"Join Us!"* box on a Group's page or Meetup page.

▲ The *"Join Us!"* button is located on the right side of your screen, just below the header banner that has the group's name on it.

Screenshot 5-9

A Group page has a description of the group and shows the "Join Us!" button.

Screenshot 5-10

A Meetup page shows the date of the Meetup and the "Join Us!" button.

Idea #111: Receiving Automatic Membership to a Meetup Group

▲ When you click the *"Join Us!"* button, some groups *will* give you automatic membership.

Screenshot 5-11

Automatic membership to join a group on Meetup.com

Idea #112: Answering Profile Questions to Join a Meetup Group

▲ When you click the *"Join Us!"* button, some groups *won't* give you automatic membership.

  ✦ You might be required to respond to a series of online profile questions before joining the group.

  ✦ Groups could have additional joining requirements that are discussed at the first Meetup you attend.

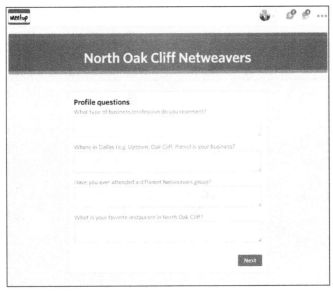

Screenshot 5-12

Sample profile questions required to join a group on Meetup.com

Idea #113: Know How to Find Members of a Meetup Group

▲ To find members of a Meetup group, go to the group's homepage.

▲ Click on *"Members"* (left column of a group page).

▲ From the *"Members"* page, view *"All Members"* or view *"The [Group's] Leadership Team."*

▲ Sort members by: *"Connection to you," "Name," "Date Joined,"* and *"Last Visited."*

Screenshot 5-13

Screenshot 5-14

To view members of a Meetup Group, click on "Members" (left column of a group's page; Screenshot 5-13). On the "Members" page, sort by "All members" or "The Leadership Team". Sort All members by: "Connections to you," "Name," "Date joined," and "Last visited" (Screenshot 5-14).

 Idea #114: Know How to Send Group Members a Message

▲ From the list of group members, locate the member you want to message.

▲ Click on the *message icon* 🗐 next to their name on the "Members" page.

Screenshot 5-15

Message members of a Meetup Group by clicking on the message icon next to their name on the "Members" page.

You can also message a member through their individual member profile.

1. Locate a member on a group's page or Meetup page.

2. Click the member's name to view the member's profile.

3. Click on the *message icon* (located under the member's name).

Idea #115: Locate the Organizer of a Meetup Group

▲ Look on the left column of any group page or Meetup page for a section that says *"Organizers."*

▲ There, you'll see the profile picture of the group's organizer and a listing of the group's co-organizers.

Screenshot 5-16

To locate a group's organizer, look on the left column of any group page or Meetup page for a section that says "Organizers."

Idea #116: Know How to View the Organizer's Meetup Profile

▲ Click on a group organizer's name to go to their profile page.

▲ On a group organizer's profile, find out their location, profession, interests, social media links, a listing of other Meetup groups they belong to, and how long they've been a group organizer.

Screenshot 5-17

A group organizer's profile on Meetup.com

Idea #117: Know How to Send a Message to the Organizer of a Meetup Group

▲ Locate the organizer of a group (See Idea #115).

▲ Click on the organizer's name.

▲ On the organizer's profile page, click the *message icon* ⊜ (under an organizer's name and title).

▲ Complete the message form and then click *"Send."*

Screenshot 5-18

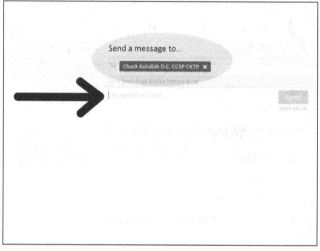

Screenshot 5-19

When sending a message to an organizer of a group, go to the organizer's profile page and click the message icon (under an organizer's name and title; Screenshot 5-18). Complete the message form and "Send a message to …" the organizer of a group (Screenshot 5-19).

 ### Idea #118: Know How to Send the Entire Leadership Team a Message through Meetup

▲ Click on the *"Contact"* button (located in the "Organizers" section of any group page or Meetup page).

▲ Complete the message form and then click, *"Send."*

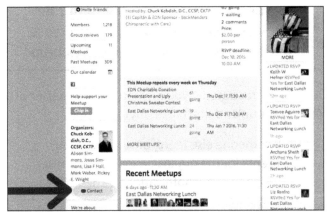

Screenshot 5-20

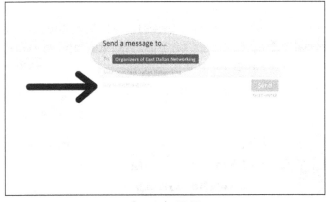

Screenshot 5-21

When sending a message to the entire leadership team of a group, click on "Contact" (located in the "Organizers" section of any group page or Meetup page; Screenshot 5-20). Complete the message form and "Send a message to …" the entire leadership team of a group (Screenshot 5-21).

Idea #119: Why You Shouldn't Be Surprised If You Do Not Receive a Response to a Message on Meetup

Do not get frustrated if you message the organizer of a Meetup Group and don't hear anything back.

▲ If someone else in the group is posting events for the organizer and the organizer has their email notifications turned off, you might not receive a reply.

▲ To ensure your message gets to an organizer, consider using another social media website.

Some organizers and attendees have links to their other social media websites on their Meetup profile page, making it easier for you to connect with them outside of Meetup.

Idea #120: Learn How To "Chip in" and Make a Voluntary Contribution to a Meetup Group

▲ Organizers can decide to take voluntary contributions from attendees on Meetup, or turn the function off.

▲ If this feature is turned on, attendees can "Chip In" by clicking the *"Chip In"* button (left side of a group page).

▲ Select the dollar amount you want to contribute.

▲ Enter your credit card information.

Screenshot 5-22

Screenshot 5-23

Screenshot 5-24

The "Chip In" button allows members to make a voluntary contribution to a Meetup group. Select "Chip In" on a group's page (Screenshot 5-22). Next, select the dollar amount you want to contribute (Screenshot 5-23) and enter your credit card information (Screenshot 5-24).

Idea #121: Understand How to Leave a Meetup Group

▲ Go to the group's page for the group you want to leave.

▲ Click *"My profile"* (upper right corner of the page).

▲ Select *"Leave this group"* from the drop-down menu.

▲ You will be asked why you want to leave the group (Response is optional).

▲ Click *"Leave the Group."*

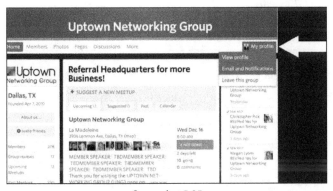

Screenshot 5-25

Screenshot 5-26

To leave a group, go to any group you've joined and click "My profile" (upper right corner of the page), and then select "Leave this group" from the drop-down menu (Screenshot 5-25). On the next page, you can tell the organizers why you are leaving the group. Then click "Leave the Group" (Screenshot 5-26).

Idea #122: Understand How to Locate All Meetup Events for a Particular City/Region

1. Click the Meetup logo (upper left corner).

2. Select the mile radius from a city and Zip Code of your choice.

3. Click the tab which says "All Meetups" (right side, above calendar).

4. Use the calendar on the page to toggle between dates.

5. Select the title of the event you're interested in attending to view the event page.

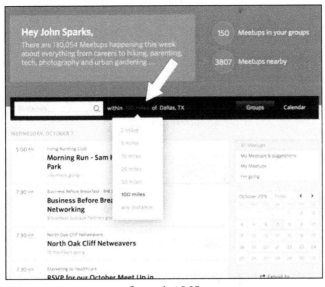

Screenshot 5-27

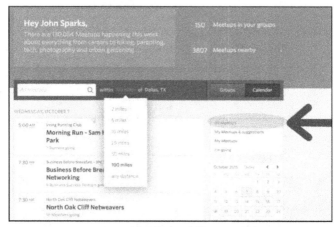

Screenshot 5-28

Screenshot 5-29

When locating all Meetup events for a particular city or region, change the mile radius, location, city, and postal code (Screenshot 5-27). Next, select "All Meetups" (Screenshot 5-28), and choose a date on the calendar you want to view events for (Screenshot 5-29).

Idea #123: Understand "Join and RSVP" And "Are You Going?" to an Event

"Join and RSVP":

▲ Click on ***"Join and RSVP"*** on a Meetup event page to both (1) join a group, and (2) RSVP for an event.

"Are You Going?":

▲ Click on *"Yes"* or *"No,"* under ***"Are You Going?"*** on a Meetup event page, when (1) you are already a member of a group, and (2) you want to RSVP for an event.

Screenshot 5-30

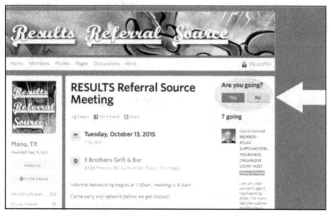

Screenshot 5-31

Click on "Join and RSVP," on a Meetup event page, to both (1) join a group, and (2) RSVP for an event (Screenshot 5-30). Click on "Yes" or "No," under "Are you going" when (1) you are already a member of a group, and (2) you want to RSVP for an event (Screenshot 5-31).

 ## Idea #124: View Meetups for Groups You Belong To

▲ Click *"Find a Meetup"* (top of the page).

▲ A list of Meetups for groups you belong to will appear.

▲ Click the title of an event and go to the event page to get more details.

▲ Follow the steps in Idea #123 to RSVP.

Screenshot 5-32

"My Meetups" shows upcoming events for groups you already belong.

 ## Idea #125: View Meetups You've Already RSVP'd For

▲ Click *"Find a Meetup"* (top of the page).

▲ Click the tab above the calendar which says "I'm going."

Screenshot 5-33

"I'm going" shows upcoming events you've already RSVP'd for.

Idea #126: Know How to Change Your RSVP for a Meetup Event

▲ See Idea #125 to find an event you have already RSVP'd to go to.

▲ Click on *"Change"* (green box, right side of screen).

▲ In the pop-up box, change your selection for "Still Going?" or "Bringing Guests?"

▲ Follow the prompts, and click *"Finish RSVP."*

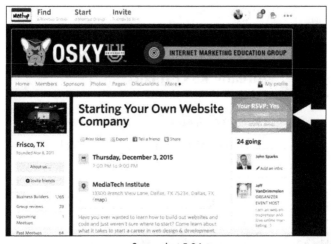

Screenshot 5-34

Screenshot 5-35

To change an RSVP, go to the page for a previously RSVP'd "Meetup." Click on "Change" in the box that says "Your RSVP: Yes" (Screenshot 5-34). In the pop-up box that appears, change your selection for "Still going?" or "Bringing guests?" (Screenshot 5-35).

 ## Idea #127: Know How to Find out Who Else Is Attending a Meetup Event

▲ Find the event page for an event you're interested in attending.

▲ In the right-hand column is a list of people who have RSVP'd they are going.

▲ Click on a member's name to view the member's Meetup profile and send them a message.

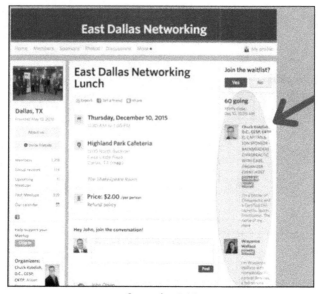

Screenshot 5-36

View a list of all attendees going to a Meetup event on a Meetup event page.

 ### Idea #128: Learn How to Adjust Your Email Settings for an Individual Meetup Group

Avoid having your email inbox flooded with emails after joining a Meetup Group. To adjust your email settings for an individual Meetup Group:

1. Go to any Meetup group you've joined.

2. Click *"My profile"* (upper right corner of the page).

3. Select *"Email and Notifications"* from the drop-down menu.

4. On the "Email Updates" page, uncheck the boxes next to the types of emails you do not wish to receive from the group.

Screenshot 5-37

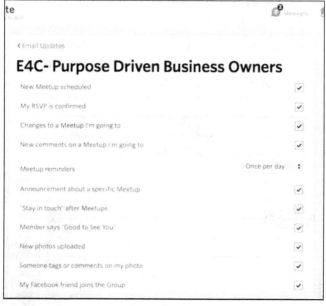

Screenshot 5-38

To adjust email updates for an individual group, go to any group you have joined. Click "My profile," followed by "Email and notifications" (Screenshot 5-37). Uncheck the boxes next to the types of emails you do not wish to receive from the group on the "Email Updates" page (Screenshot 5-38).

Idea #129: Understand Another Way to Adjust Your Email Settings for ALL Meetup Groups and Individual Meetup Groups

1. Click your profile picture (top right corner of the screen).
2. Select "Settings" from the drop-down menu.
3. Click *"Email Updates"* on the General settings page.

From the "Email Updates" page: (1) toggle email frequency for ALL your messages, or (2) scroll down and toggle the email frequency for individual groups.

Screenshot 5-39

Screenshot 5-40

Screenshot 5-41

Updates about your groups

The Architecture Happy Hour   Edit

Arlington Social Media Marketing Group   Edit

Austin Digital Marketing Meetup   Edit

Austin Inventopreneurs (Inventors & Entrepreneurs)   Edit

Austin Online Marketing Club   Edit

Austin Small Business Owners Meetup   Edit

The Austin WordPress Meetup Group   Edit

BigDOCC - Talking Tech, Startups, and the Digital Lifestyle!   Edit

BizLink Business Development, Networking & Speaker Assoc.   Edit

Brainstorming Networkers Meetup   Edit

Christian Business Nurturing   Edit

Screenshot 5-42

To adjust your emails for ALL groups, click your profile picture (top right corner of the screen) and select "Settings" from the drop-down menu (Screenshot 5-39). On the General settings page, click on "Email Updates" (Screenshot 5-40). On the "Email Updates" page, click "Turn off" where it says "Email updates are on" (Screenshot 5-41). Scroll down on the "Email Updates" page to find another place where you can adjust the email settings for your individual groups (Screenshot 5-42).

Idea #130: Know Where to Go to Get More Help with the Meetup Website

<u>Help.meetup.com</u> is the best place to go to get more help with <u>Meetup.com</u> including:

▲ Hosting, organizing, and managing Meetup groups

▲ Managing your account

▲ Troubleshooting

▲ Privacy and safety

▲ Legal resources

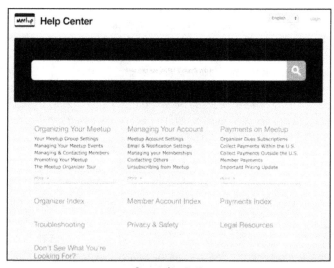

Screenshot 5-43

Meetup Help Center at <u>help.Meetup.com</u>

PART 6

Meetup on the Go with the Meetup App

 Idea #131: Know How to Find Groups You Already Belong to Using the Meetup App

---

▲ Select *"Groups"* (bottom menu bar).

▲ A listing of groups you're already a member of will appear under the section heading: *"Your Meetup Groups."*

Screenshot 6-1

*Select "Groups" (bottom menu bar) to get to the "Groups" page
on the Meetup app.*

 ## Idea #132: Know How to Search for New Groups Using the Meetup App

▲ Select "Groups" 🏴 (bottom menu bar).

▲ Click the *search icon* 🔍 (upper right corner of the page).

   ✦ Search groups by suggested categories.

   ✦ Search groups by typing your own keywords into the search box.

✦ Search groups within a certain mile
   radius of a city by clicking on the city
   name.

Screenshot 6-2   *Screenshot 6-3*

*Search for groups within a certain distance of a city by clicking
on the city name (Screenshot 6-2) and then adjusting location
and mile radius (Screenshot 6-3).*

Idea #133: Know How to Find the Description of a Group Using the Meetup App

▲ Use Idea #131 and #132 to find a group page you are interested in.

▲ On the group's page, click the group's main header image, or click "*more info*" (lower right corner of the main header image). A full description of the group will appear.

Screenshot 6-4   Screenshot 6-5

To find the description of a group, go to a group's page you are interested in. Click the main header image for the group, or click "more info" (lower right corner of the main header image; Screenshot 6-4). A full description of the group will appear (Screenshot 6-5).

Idea #134: Learn How to Join a New Group Using The "+Add Me" Button on the Meetup App

▲ Find a group's page you are interested in.

▲ Click the "+Add Me" button to join the group.

▲ Some groups *will* automatically grant you membership.

  ✦ *"Welcome!"* will appear after you click the *"+Add Me"* button.

▲ Some groups *will not* automatically grant you membership.

  ✦ You might be required to upload a photo or take a new photo from your device. If this happens, membership will be pending the group organizer's approval.

  ✦ You might be required to "Introduce Yourself" by responding to a series of profile questions before you can join the group.

  ✦ Groups could have additional joining requirements that are discussed at the first Meetup you attend.

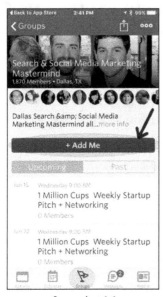

Screenshot 6-6

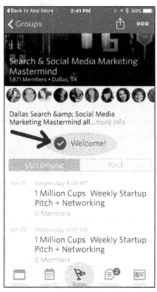

Screenshot 6-7

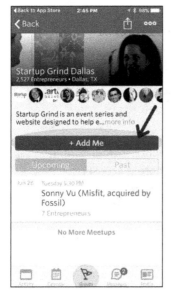

Screenshot 6-8

Screenshot 6-9

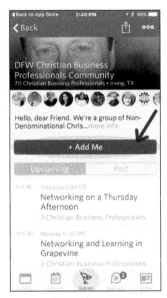

Screenshot 6-10   Screenshot 6-11

After clicking "+Add Me" (Screenshot 6-6, Screenshot 6-8, and Screenshot 6-10) you will either (1) receive a welcome message which means you are now a member of the group (Screenshot 6-7), (2) receive instructions to either select a photo from your photo album or take a new picture using your device (Screenshot 6-9), or (3) be prompted to "Introduce Yourself" and respond to a series of profile questions (Screenshot 6-11). If asked to choose a photo from your photo album or asked to respond to a series of profile questions, membership to the group will be pending the group organizer's approval.

Idea #135: Know How to Find Members of a Meetup Group Using the Meetup App

▲ Click any of the profile pictures at the top of a group's page.

    ✦ You will be shown a list of all group members for a particular Meetup group.

Screenshot 6-12   *Screenshot 6-13*

Click any of the profile pictures at the top of a group's page (Screenshot 6-12), to view a list of all the group members of a Meetup group (Screenshot 6-13).

Idea #136: View the Profile of Specific Members of a Meetup Group Using the Meetup App

▲ After accessing the list of all group members from a group's page, click anywhere in the box of a user to view their profile.

Screenshot 6-14   *Screenshot 6-15*

Select a user from a list of all group members (Screenshot 6-14) to view their profile (Screenshot 6-15).

Idea #137: Learn How to Send a Message to Specific Members of a Meetup Group Using the Meetup App

▲ Locate the profile of the user you want to send a message to using the Meetup app.

▲ Click the word *"Message"* on the user's profile page.

▲ Type your message, and click *"Post."*

Screenshot 6-16   Screenshot 6-17

Selecting "Message" on a group member's profile (Screenshot 6-16) allows you to send a message to the user (Screenshot 6-17).

Idea #138: Understand How to Share A "Group" Page with Others

▲ Find the page for the group you want to share.

▲ To share a group's page, click the the *share icon* 🖸 (right corner of the screen).

▲ Follow the prompts to share via AirDrop, Facebook, Twitter, Pinterest, Google+, Facebook Messenger, SMS (text message), or email.

Screenshot 6-18

Screenshot 6-19

Click the share icon (right corner; Screenshot 6-18) to share a group's page via AirDrop, Facebook, Twitter, Pinterest, Google+, Facebook Messenger, SMS (text message), or email (Screenshot 6-19).

Idea #139: Learn How to "Chip In" and Make a Contribution to a Meetup Group on the Meetup App

1. Click the menu button represented by three dots ••• (upper right corner of the screen).

2. Select "Chip In" from the drop-down menu.

3. Choose a dollar amount to contribute.

4. Add your credit card information.

5. See Idea #120 for more things to know before using "Chip In" on the Meetup app.

Screenshot 6-20   *Screenshot 6-21*

Screenshot 6-22   *Screenshot 6-23*

Click the menu button represented by three dots (upper right corner of the screen; Screenshot 6-20), and select "Chip in" (Screenshot 6-21) to make a donation to a group. Select a dollar amount you want to contribute (Screenshot 6-22), and add your credit card information (Screenshot 6-23).

Idea #140: Learn How to Leave a Meetup Group on the Meetup App

▲ Find the "Group" page for the group you want to leave.

▲ Click the menu button represented by three dots ⋯ (upper right corner of the screen).

▲ Select *"Leave this Group."*

▲ When the pop-up appears, confirm you want to leave the group.

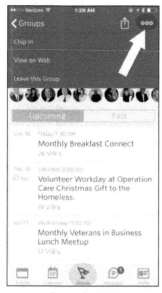

Screenshot 6-24

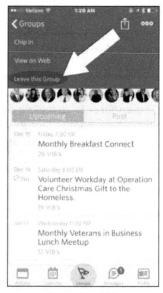

Screenshot 6-25

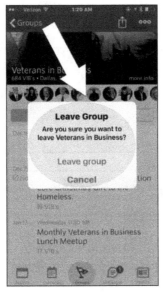

Screenshot 6-26

To leave a group, find the group you want to leave. Click the menu button represented by three dots (upper right corner of the screen; Screenshot 6-24). Select "Leave this Group" (Screenshot 6-25). When the pop-up appears, confirm you want to leave the group (Screenshot 6-26).

 **Idea #141:
Sort Meetup Events**

Meetups can be sorted and filtered by:

▲ ***"All Meetups Nearby"***: Meetups nearby.

▲ ***"My Meetups And Suggestions"***:
   Suggested Meetups.

▲ ***"My Meetups"***: Event listings for groups you're a member of but have not RSVP'd to.

▲ ***"I'm Going"***: Meetups you've already RSVP'd to.

▲ ***"I went"***: Meetups already attended.

Follow these steps:

▲ Click the *"Calendar" button* 📅 (bottom menu bar).

▲ Click the *slider icon* ⚏ (upper left corner).

▲ Sort Meetup events by selecting either: *"All Meetups nearby," "My Meetups & suggestions," "My Meetups," "I'm going," or "I went."*

Screenshot 6-27   *Screenshot 6-28*

Screenshot 6-29

To sort and view event listings, click the "Calendar" button (bottom menu bar; Screenshot 6-27), followed by the slider icon (upper left corner, Screenshot 6-28). After, choose from "All Meetups nearby," "My Meetups & suggestions," "My Meetups," "I'm going," or "I went" (Screenshot 6-29).

 ## Idea #142: Search for Meetup Events by Location and Category

▲ Click the *Calendar button* 📅 (bottom menu bar).

▲ Click the search icon 🔍 (upper right corner of the "Calendar" page).

✦ Select the city name (top of the "Search" page) to change the mile radius and the target location of the events you are searching.

✦ Search events by either suggested categories, or by custom categories (typing keywords into the search box).

Screenshot 6-30

Screenshot 6-31

Screenshot 6-32   Screenshot 6-33

Click the "Calendar" button (bottom menu bar; Screenshot 6-30), followed by the search icon (upper right corner; Screenshot 6-31), to search for events by location and category. Select the city name (top of the screen; Screenshot 6-32) to change the mile radius and the target location of the events you are searching (Screenshot 6-33).

 ## Idea #143: Find the Description for an Event Using the Meetup App

▲ See Idea #141 and #142 to find an event.

▲ After finding and clicking on the event you wish to look at, click *"more info"* (under the event title, date, and location) to get more information about the event and the group hosting the event.

After reading information about the event, or the group hosting the event, you can:

▲ Add the event to your calendar

▲ View a map showing the event location

▲ RSVP

▲ Add comments and photos for the event

▲ See who is hosting/organizing the event

▲ See who is going to the event

Screenshot 6-34   *Screenshot 6-35*

Click "more info," on a Meetup event page (under event title, date, and location; Screenshot 6-34). More information about the event or the group hosting the event will appear (Screenshot 6-35).

Idea #144: Understand How "Join and RSVP" And "Are You Going?" to an Event Works Using the Meetup App

▲ Click the *"Join and RSVP"* button on any Meetup event page on the Meetup app to (1) join the group, and (2) RSVP for an event.

▲ Click the red "RSVP" button on a Meetup event page on the Meetup app when (1) you are already a member of a group, and (2) you want to RSVP for an event.

▲ Next, select the number of guests you are bringing.

▲ Slide the calendar switch from "Off" to "On" to add the event to your calendar.

▲ Click the green *"RSVP"* button.

Screenshot 6-36   Screenshot 6-37

Click the red "RSVP" button on a Meetup event page on the Meetup app when (1) you are already a member of a group, and (2) you want to RSVP for an event. (Screenshot 6-36). Next, on the RSVP page, select the number of guests you are bringing, and choose if you want to add the event to the calendar. Click the green "RSVP" button to submit your response (Screenshot 6-37).

Idea #145: Know How to Change Your RSVP for a Meetup Event

▲ Locate an event you've previously RSVP'd for.

▲ Click anywhere on the gray bar that says *"Your RSVP: Yes."*

▲ On the RSVP page, change *"Will You Be There?"* from *"Yes"* to *"No."* Also, change the number of guests you are bringing.

▲ Add the event to your calendar if you choose.

▲ After making your changes, click the green *"RSVP"* button.

Screenshot 6-38

Screenshot 6-39

Screenshot 6-40

To change your reservation, locate a previously RSVP'd event. Select "Your RSVP: Yes" (Screenshot 6-38). Change "Will You Be There?" from "Yes" to "No," or change the number of guests you are bringing (Screenshot 6-39). Click the green "RSVP" button to submit your response (Screenshot 6-40).

 Idea #146: Learn How to Find the Page for a Group That Is Hosting an Event

For an Event You Have *Not* RSVP'd for:

▲ Click the *"Calendar" button* 📅 (bottom menu bar).

▲ Click the *slider icon* 🎚 (upper left corner).

▲ Select either:

   ✦ *"All Meetups Nearby."*

   ✦ *"My Meetups And Suggestions."*

   ✦ *"My Meetups" (Listing of events for groups you are already a member of but have not yet RSVP'd for).*

▲ Locate and then click the name of the event you want to view.

   ✦ The event page for the event will appear.

   ✦ The name of the group hosting an event will appear above the name of the event (top of the screen).

▲ Click on the name of the group.

   ✦ You will be taken to a page to view the group hosting the event.

▲ Click the main header image for the group (top of the page), or click *"more info"* (at the end of the abbreviated description of the group).

   ✦ A full description of the group will appear.

Screenshot 6-41

Screenshot 6-42

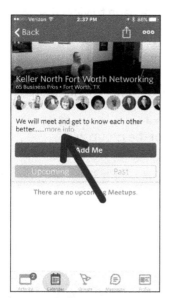

Screenshot 6-43

Screenshot 6-44

To get to a group's page from an event page, for an event you have not already RSVP'd to, locate the event by clicking on the "Calendar" button and searching for it in calendar view. Click the name of the event (Screenshot 6-41). The event page will appear. At the top of the event page, above the name of the event, the group name and a right arrow will appear. Click the name of the group (Screenshot 6-42). The group page will appear. Click the main header image for the group (top of the page), or click "more info" (at the end of the abbreviated description of the group; Screenshot 6-43). A full description of the group will appear (Screenshot 6-44).

For an Event You Have Already RSVP'd for, Or Already Attended:

▲ Click the *"Calendar" button* 📅 (bottom menu bar).

▲ Click the *slider icon* ⚏ (upper left corner).

▲ Select either:

  ✦ *"I'm Going" (Meetups you have already RSVP'd for).*

  ✦ *"I went" (Meetups already attended).*

▲ Locate and then click the name of the event you want to view.

  ✦ The event page for the event will appear.

  ✦ The event page should have a gray bar in the center that says "Your RSVP: Yes."

  ✦ The name of the group hosting the event will appear above the event name (top of the screen).

▲ Click on the name of the group.

  ✦ You will be taken to a page to view the group hosting the event.

▲ Click the main header image for the group (top of the page), or click *"more info"* (lower right corner of the main header image).

  ✦ A full description of the group will appear.

Screenshot 6-45

Screenshot 6-46

Screenshot 6-47

To get to a group page from an event page, for an event you have already RSVP'd to, locate the event in calendar view. Click the name of the event. The event page will appear. The event page should have a gray bar in the center that says "Your RSVP: Yes." At the top of the event page, above the name of the event, the group name and a right arrow will appear. Click the name of the group (Screenshot 6-45). The group page will appear. Click the main header image for the group (top of the page), or click "more info" (lower right corner of the main header image; Screenshot 6-46). A full description of the group will appear (Screenshot 6-47).

Idea #147: Learn How to Share Details about an Event Using the Meetup App

▲ Locate the event page you want to share.

▲ Click the *share icon* 📤 (right corner of the screen).

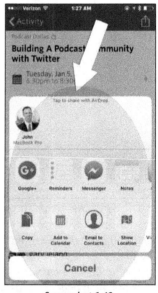

Screenshot 6-48   *Screenshot 6-49*

Click the share icon (right corner; Screenshot 6-48) to share an event using AirDrop, Facebook, Twitter, Pinterest, Google+, Facebook Messenger, SMS (text message), or email (Screenshot 6-49).

Idea #148: Locate the Organizer of a Meetup Event through the Meetup App

▲ Follow Ideas #141 and #142 to find a Meetup event page.

▲ Scroll down on an event page and look under the section that reads: *"[NUMBER] HOSTING."*

✦ These are the organizers of the group.

Screenshot 6-50

To locate the organizer(s) of an event, find the section on a Meetup event page that reads "[NUMBER] HOSTING" (Screenshot 6-50).

Idea #149:
View the Organizer's Profile

▲ Follow the steps in Idea #148 to find the organizers of a group.

▲ Click anywhere on their name or picture to view their profile page.

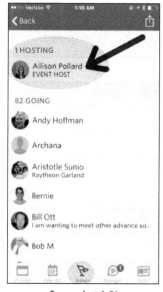

Screenshot 6-51

Screenshot 6-52

Choose an organizer's name, from the list of attendees (Screenshot 6-51), to view the organizer's profile page (Screenshot 6-52).

Idea #150: Send the Organizer of a Meetup Group a Message

▲ Follow Ideas #148 and #149 to find an organizer's profile page.

▲ Click the word *"Message,"* on the organizer's profile page.

▲ Type your message to the organizer, and click *"Post."*

Screenshot 6-53

Screenshot 6-54

Select "Message," on an organizer's profile page (Screenshot 6-53), to send a message to the organizer (Screenshot 6-54).

Idea #151:
Find out Who's Going to an Event

▲ Go to any Meetup event page.

▲ Scroll down.

▲ Find the section that reads: *"[NUMBER] GOING."*

▲ These are the attendees who have RSVP'd.

| Screenshot 6-55 | Screenshot 6-56 |

Scroll down the event detail page of any Meetup event (Screenshot 6-55), to view who's RSVP'd for an event (Screenshot 6-56).

Idea #152: Know How to View Profiles of Those Attending Meetup Events

1. Follow the steps in Idea #151 to find out who's going to an event.

2. Click anywhere on an attendee's name or picture.

3. View the attendee's profile.

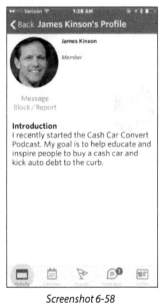

Screenshot 6-57   *Screenshot 6-58*

Select an attendee who's RSVP'd for an event (Screenshot 6-57) to view their profile (Screenshot 6-58).

Idea #153: Know How to Send a Message to Someone Attending an Event

▲ Follow the steps in Ideas #151 and #152 to find out who is attending an event and view their profile.

▲ Click on the word *"Message",* on an attendee's profile page.

▲ Type a message to the attendee.

▲ Click *"Post."*

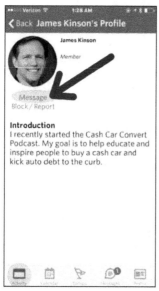

Screenshot 6-59   *Screenshot 6-60*

Select "Message" on an event attendee's profile who has RSVP'd for an event (Screenshot 6-59) to send them a message (Screenshot 6-60).

Idea #154: Know the Difference between Messages on the Meetup App and the Web-Based Version

▲ Users cannot send messages to an entire leadership team on the Meetup app.

✦ Users are only able to send messages to individual users.

▲ Users can send messages to multiple users or groups on the web-based version.

▲ Users can send messages to the entire leadership team on the web-based version.

See Idea #118 to message the entire leadership team using the web-based version.

Idea #155: Adjust Settings, Notifications, and Email Settings for ALL Meetup Groups on the Meetup App

1. Click the *"Profile" button* 👤 (right-hand corner, on the bottom menu bar).

2. Select *"Settings."*

✦ Adjust push notifications, email updates, privacy settings, and other settings here.

3. Choose "*Email Updates.*"

    ✦ Turn on/off email updates for all
       groups (Screenshot 6-63), or turn
       on/off email updates for messages
       received on Meetup (Screenshot 6-64).

Screenshot 6-61

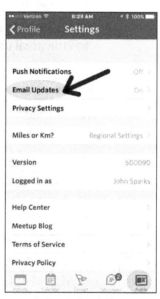

Screenshot 6-62

Screenshot 6-63   Screenshot 6-64

To adjust settings, notifications, and email settings, for all Meetup groups, select the "Profile" button, and then select "Settings" (Screenshot 6-61). Next, click "Email Updates" (Screenshot 6-62), to turn on/off email updates from all groups (Screenshot 6-63), or turn on/off email updates for messages received on Meetup (Screenshot 6-64).

 Idea #156: Understand How to Adjust Your Email Settings for Individual Meetup Groups

▲ To turn emails off for individual groups, click the *"Profile" button* 📧 (right-hand corner, bottom menu bar).

▲ Click *"Settings."*

▲ Click on *"Email updates."*

▲ Scroll down and locate the section that says *"Updates About Your Groups."*

   ✦ In this section, you will see a list of names for each group you belong to.

▲ Click the name of a group.

▲ Adjust the email settings for the group you select.

Screenshot 6-65

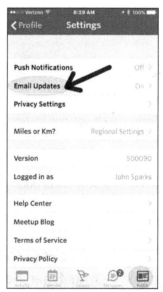

Screenshot 6-66

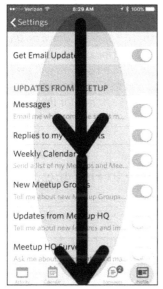

Screenshot 6-67

Screenshot 6-68

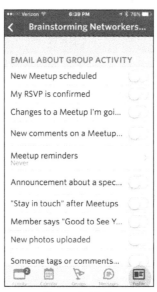

Screenshot 6-69

To adjust email settings for individual Meetup groups, click the "Profile" button and then select "Settings" (Screenshot 6-65). Next, click "Email Updates" (Screenshot 6-66). Scroll down on the screen that appears (Screenshot 6-67) and locate a section that says "Updates About Your Groups." In this section, you will see a list of names for each group you belong to. Click the name of a group (Screenshot 6-68). Adjust the email settings for the group you select (Screenshot 6-69).

 ### Idea #157: Know How to Find the Meetup "Help Center"

▲ Click the *"Profile" button* 🖼 (right-hand corner, on the bottom menu bar).

▲ Select *"Settings."*

▲ Select *"Help Center."*

Screenshot 6-70

Screenshot 6-71

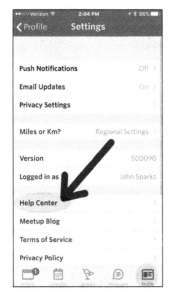

Screenshot 6-72

Screenshot 6-73

To access the Meetup "Help Center," click the "Profile" button on any page (right-hand corner, bottom menu bar; Screenshot 6-70). Click "Settings" on the profile page (Screenshot 6-71). In settings, click "Help Center" (Screenshot 6-72). Enter a topic or question to search for in the Meetup "Help Center" (Screenshot 6-73).

PART 7
Locate Events the Easy Way with Eventbrite

 Idea #158:
Try out Eventbrite

Eventbrite is another great place to find networking events.

- ▲ Eventbrite is a meeting exchange network, and self-service ticketing platform, which lists events in 187 countries.

- ▲ Organizers can list both free and paid events on Eventbrite. The website makes a percentage of the ticket price for all paid events.

- ▲ Attendees can search for events with the name of an event, location, date, or any combination of the three.

Screenshot 7-1

Homepage on Eventbrite.com

▲ **Eventbrite is available on the web at:**

https://play.google.com/store/apps/
details?id=com.eventbrite.attendee&hl=en

▲ **iPhone users can download the Eventbrite app by going to:**

https://itunes.apple.com/us/
app/eventbrite-local-events-fun/
id487922291?mt=8

▲ **Android users can download the Eventbrite app by going to:**

https://play.google.com/store/apps/
details?id=com.eventbrite.attendee&hl=en

Screenshot 7-2

Eventbrite app in the Apple iTunes Store.

 Idea #159: Understand How to Search for Events with Eventbrite

▲ On a desktop or laptop, go to http://www.Eventbrite.com

▲ Log in, or sign up for the site.

▲ Type in the name or category of the event, city/location, and date of the event.

▲ Click the blue "*Search*" button.

▲ Events matching the search criteria will appear.

Screenshot 7-3

Search for events by date and location on <u>Eventbrite.com</u>

 ## Idea #160: Be Familiar with How to Change the View of Event Listings

▲ View events in either list view or grid view.

▲ Click the *list view icon* ≡ or *grid view icon* ▦ (upper right of an event listings page) to change from list view to grid view or vice versa.

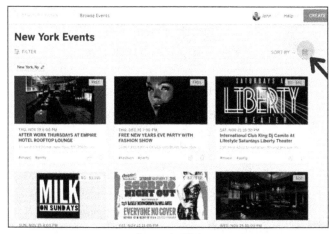

Screenshot 7-4

Screenshot 7-5

To change views from grid view to list view, select the list view icon (Screenshot 7-4). To change views from list view to grid view, select the grid view icon (Screenshot 7-5).

Idea #161: Search for Events by Category, Event Type, Date, or Price in Grid View

▲ Select *"FILTER"* (upper left of the screen under location) in grid view to search events by: category, event type, date, and price.

▲ Select the *down arrow* ❤ (located to the right of *"SORT BY"* in the upper right of the screen) in grid view to sort events by relevance or date.

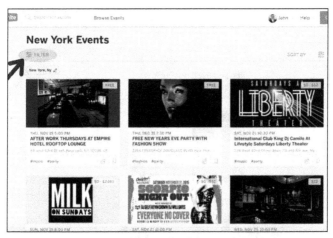

Screenshot 7-6

Screenshot 7-7

Screenshot 7-8

In grid view, select "FILTER" (upper left of the screen under city/ location; Screenshot 7-6). A pop-up box will appear, allowing you to search by: category, event type, date, and price (Screenshot 7-7). Select the down arrow (located to the right of "SORT BY" in the upper right of the screen) in grid view to sort events by relevance or date (Screenshot 7-8).

Idea #162: Search for Events by Category, Event Type, Date, or Price in List View

▲ Use drop-down sub-categories in list view to search by: category, event type, date, and price (left side of the screen).

▲ Use the *"RELEVANCE"* and *"DATE"* tabs to sort by relevance or date (right side of the screen next to the *grid view icon* 🔡).

Screenshot 7-9

Screenshot 7-10

In list view, use drop-down sub-categories to search by: category, event type, date, and price (left side of the screen; Screenshot 7-9). Sort events by relevance or date by clicking on the "Relevance" or "Date" tabs (upper right of the screen next to the grid view icon; Screenshot 7-10).

 ## Idea #163: Use the Eventbrite Website to See an Event Detail Page

▲ Click any event in grid view or list view to view an event detail page for the event.

▲ On an event detail page:

✦ View a map showing the exact location of the event.

✦ "Save This Event."

✦ Add it to your calendar.

✦ "Register" (purchase tickets).

✦ Share the event on social media.

✦ Get an event description.

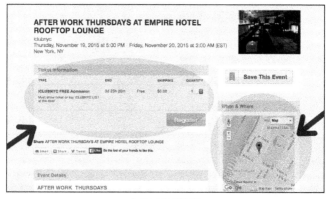

Screenshot 7-11

On an event detail page: view a map of the event, "Save This Event," add it to your calendar, "Register" (purchase tickets), share the event on social media, and get an event description.

 ## Idea #164: Understand How Saving an Event Works

▲ Saving an event makes it easier to find later by bookmarking it.

▲ Saving an event does not hold a ticket or space at an event.

▲ The only guarantee of getting into any event is by purchasing a ticket.

Idea #165: Two Ways to Save an Event for Future Reference

There are two ways to save an event for future reference:

1. Click the *bookmark icon* 🔖 (lower right corner of any event listing in grid view).

   ✦ The *bookmark icon* 🔖 will change from white to blue.

2. Click the *"Save This Event"* button on the event detail page.

   ✦ This allows you to view how many others have also saved the event.

Screenshot 7-12

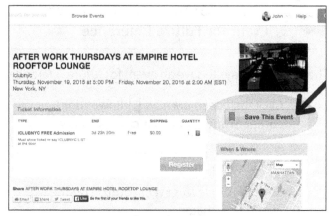

Screenshot 7-13

There are two ways to save an event for future reference. One of the ways is by clicking the bookmark icon (lower right corner of any event listing in grid view; Screenshot 7-12). A second way is to click the "Save This Event" button on the event detail page (Screenshot 7-13).

 ## Idea #166: Understand How to View Saved Events

▲ Click the *down arrow* ❤ (located to the right of your profile picture and username; upper right of the screen) on any Eventbrite page.

▲ Select "Saved" from the drop-down menu and go to the "Saved" events page.

✦ Only bookmarked events that haven't
   happened yet are displayed on the
   "Saved" events page.

✦ Saved events on the web-based
   version will sync with the mobile app.

✦ Once an event ends, it will no longer
   appear on the *"Saved"* events page.

Screenshot 7-14

Screenshot 7-15

To view your "Saved" events, click the down arrow (located to the right of your profile picture and username; upper right of the screen; Screenshot 7-14). Next, select "Saved" from the drop-down menu. Your "Saved" events will appear (Screenshot 7-15).

Idea #167: View Event Listings for Events You've Already Purchased Tickets for (Upcoming and past Events)

▲ Click the *down arrow* ❤ (located to the right of your profile picture and username) in the upper right of any Eventbrite page.

▲ Select *"Tickets"* from the drop-down menu.

✦ Upcoming events and past events are displayed on the web-version.

✦ Only upcoming events are displayed on the mobile app.

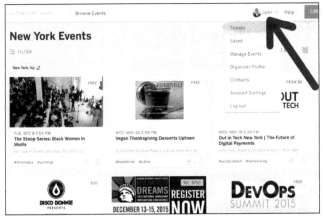

Screenshot 7-16

Screenshot 7-17

To view event listings for events you've already purchased tickets for (upcoming and past events), click the down arrow (located to the right of your profile picture and username) in the upper right of any Eventbrite page (Screenshot 7-16). Next, select "Tickets" from the drop-down menu. The "Tickets" page will appear where you can view RSVP'd events and tickets already purchased for both upcoming and past events (Screenshot 7-17).

Idea #168: Learn What You Can Do from The "Tickets" Page for Upcoming Events

Click on an upcoming event you've already purchased tickets for on the *"Tickets"* page to:

1. Print tickets

2. Cancel an order

3. Contact the organizer

Screenshot 7-18

Screenshot 7-19

Click any event on the "Tickets" page (Screenshot 7-18) to be taken to a page where you can: print tickets, cancel an order for previously purchased tickets, or contact the organizer of an event (Screenshot 7-19).

 ## Idea #169: Learn What You Can Do from The "Tickets" Page for Past Events

On the "Tickets" page, click on a past event you purchased tickets for and:

1. View a receipt of purchase for the event.

2. Contact the organizer.

Screenshot 7-20

On the "Tickets" page, click on a past event you've purchased tickets for and view a receipt for the event or contact the organizer.

 ## Idea #170:
Share Events via Eventbrite

▲   Click the *share icon* 🔗 in grid view to share an event on: Facebook, Facebook Messenger, LinkedIn, Twitter, or email. (See Screenshot 7-21).

▲   Also click the *share icon* 🔗 to populate a link for the event that you can share on other social media sites.

Screenshot 7-21

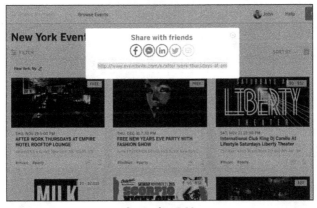

Screenshot 7-22

Click the share icon (Screenshot 7-21) at the bottom of each event in grid view to share upcoming events on: Facebook, Facebook Messenger, LinkedIn, Twitter, or email (Screenshot 7-22). Also, click the share icon (Screenshot 7-21) to populate a link, for the event, that you can share on other social media sites (located under the social media icons; Screenshot 7-22).

Idea #171: Understand How to Request a Refund and Cancel an Eventbrite RSVP

For a paid event:

▲ "Contact The Organizer" to request a refund.

For an unpaid event:

▲ Click the *down arrow* ❤ (located to the right of your profile picture and username) in the upper right corner of any Eventbrite page.

▲ Select *"Tickets"* from the drop-down menu.

▲ Choose the event with which you wish to cancel the RSVP.

▲ Click "Cancel Order," and confirm your selection.

Screenshot 7-23

Screenshot 7-24

Screenshot 7-25

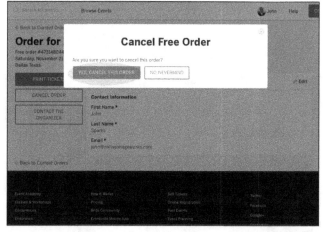

Screenshot 7-26

To cancel an RSVP for an event that has not yet been paid, click the down arrow (located to the right of your profile picture and username; upper right of the screen; Screenshot 7-23). Next, select "Tickets" from the drop-down menu. Select the event you want to cancel your RSVP to (Screenshot 7-24). On the detail page for the event, select "Cancel Order" (Screenshot 7-25). Next, confirm you want to cancel the free order (Screenshot 7-26).

Idea #172: Know How to Get to "Eventbrite Support"

▲ "Eventbrite Support" is Eventbrite's help and support forum.

▲ To access "Eventbrite Support," go to https://www.eventbrite.com/support

▲ Also access "Eventbrite Support" by clicking the *down arrow* ∨ (located to the right of the word "Help"; upper right corner of the screen) on any Eventbrite page.

"Eventbrite Support" topics include:

▲ Hosting, organizing, and managing your own events.

▲ Setting up your organizer profile page.

▲ Using promotional tools.

▲ Publishing your event to Facebook.

▲ Setting up a repeating event schedule.

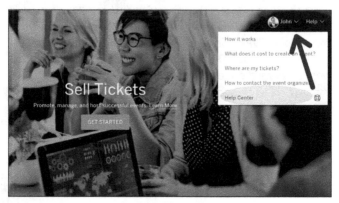

Screenshot 7-27

Screenshot 7-28

To get to "Eventbrite Support," click the down arrow (located to the right of the word "Help"; upper right corner of the screen) on any Eventbrite page (Screenshot 7-27). "Eventbrite Support" will appear (Screenshot 7-28).

PART 8

Take Networking Mobile with the Eventbrite App

 Idea #173: Learn How to Discover Events by Location Using the Eventbrite App

1. Click the *"Discover"* button 🅔 (bottom menu bar).

2. Click the upside-down triangle (next to the city name; top center of the screen) to change the location.

   ✦ Use your "Current Location."

   ✦ Pick from "Popular Locations."

   ✦ Manually enter a location of choice.

3. Swipe your phone screen to the left and view:

    ✦ "Recommended" events.

    ✦ "Popular" events.

    ✦ Events "This Weekend."

    ✦ View events your "Friends" are attending.

    ✦ Events "Nearby."

4. Scroll up and down under each tab to scan event listings.

    ✦ The price for each event is listed on the top right of each event photo.

5. Click on each event listing to view an event detail page for the event.

Screenshot 8-1

Screenshot 8-2

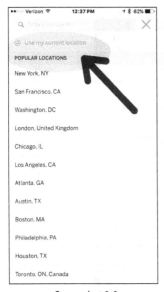

Screenshot 8-3   Screenshot 8-4

Screenshot 8-5   Screenshot 8-6

Screenshot 8-7

To search and sort events, click the "Discover" button (bottom menu bar; Screenshot 8-1). Click the upside-down triangle (next to the city name; top center of the screen) to change the location (Screenshot 8-2). Search for events by current location or by popular locations (Screenshot 8-3). Users can also search for events by manually typing in a location (Screenshot 8-4). On the Discover page, swipe your phone screen to the left and choose to view events by: "Recommended," "Popular," etc. (Screenshot 8-5). The price for each event is listed on the top right of each event photo (Screenshot 8-6). Click on each event listing to view an event detail page for the event (Screenshot 8-7).

Idea #174: Understand How to Search for Events by Category Using the Eventbrite App

▲ Click the *"Search"* button 🔍 (bottom menu bar).

✦ Choose from a list of Eventbrite categories to search, or click the *search icon* 🔍 (inside the "Search Events" box; upper left corner of the screen) to do a custom search.

▲ Click on the *"Current Location"* ◎ box (to the right of the *"Current Location"* icon) to search using your "current location," "popular locations," or manually enter a location of choice.

✦ See Idea #173 for another way to discover and search events by location.

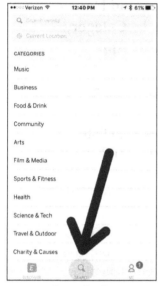

Screenshot 8-8

Screenshot 8-9

Screenshot 8-10

To search for an event by category using the Eventbrite app, click the "Search" button (bottom menu bar; Screenshot 8-8). Choose from a list of Eventbrite categories to search or click the search icon (inside the "Search Events" box; upper left corner of the screen; Screenshot 8-9) to do a custom search and manually type in the category name (Screenshot 8-10). Click on the "Current Location" box (to the right of the "Current Location" icon) to search using your "current location," "popular locations," or manually enter a location of choice.

Idea #175: Understand How to Use the Eventbrite App to Find Events Which Match Your Interests

▲ Click the *"Me"* button ⚇ (bottom menu bar).

▲ Swipe your phone screen to the left to view the tab that says *"Interests."*

▲ Select and choose your interests (e.g. Music, Business, Food and Drink, Community, Arts, etc.).

▲ Click the *"Discover"* button 🄴 (bottom menu bar).

▲ Swipe your phone screen to the left to view the tab that says *"Recommended."*

▲ The *"Recommended"* tab is where you'll view the events that match your selected interests.

Screenshot 8-11

Screenshot 8-12

Screenshot 8-13

To find events that match your interests on Eventbrite, click the "Me" button (bottom menu bar; Screenshot 8-11). Swipe your phone screen to the left to view the tab that says "Interests" (Screenshot 8-12). Choose and select your interests from the menu (Screenshot 8-13). Click "Discover" (bottom menu bar), and then swipe your phone screen to the left to view the tab that says "Recommended" to view the events that match your selected interests.

Idea #176: Know How to Share Events You Have Not RSVP'd or Purchased Tickets for Using the Eventbrite App

1. Click the *"Discover"* button and locate the event.

2. Click the *share icon* 📤 (lower right corner of each event listing).

3. Select to share the event via:

   ✦ SMS (text message)

   ✦ Email

   ✦ Link created by Eventbrite

   ✦ Facebook

   ✦ Twitter

OR:

1. Go to an event detail page for an event.

2. Once inside the event detail page, click the share icon 🔼 (upper right corner).

3. Select to share the event via:

   ✦ SMS (text message)

   ✦ Email

   ✦ Link created by Eventbrite

   ✦ Facebook

   ✦ Twitter

Screenshot 8-14   *Screenshot 8-15*

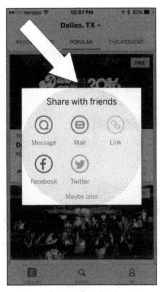

Screenshot 8-16

When sharing an event using the Eventbrite app, click the "Discover" button (Screenshot 8-14). Locate the event listing to share, and click the share icon (lower right corner of each event listing; Screenshot 8-15). Choose to share the event by: SMS (text message), email, etc. (Screenshot 8-16).

Screenshot 8-17

Screenshot 8-18

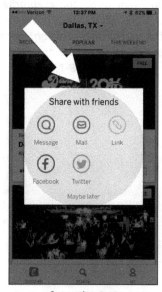

Screenshot 8-19

A second way to share an event using the Eventbrite app, is to click the "Discover" button (Screenshot 8-17). Locate the event listing to share, and click on it and go to the event detail page. Next, click the share icon (upper right corner; Screenshot 8-18). Choose to share the event by: SMS (text message), email, etc. (Screenshot 8-19).

Idea #177: Know How to Save Events and View Previously Saved Events Using the Eventbrite App

Similar to the web version, saving an event on the Eventbrite app does not hold a ticket for an event. The only guarantee of getting into an event is by purchasing a ticket.

1. Click the *"Discover"* button 🅴 and locate the event.

2. Click the *bookmark icon* 🔖 to save an event (lower right corner of each event listing, next to the *share icon* 📤).

    ✦ Bookmarked events, which have not happened yet, are displayed on the *"Saved"* events page.

    ✦ Saved events on the mobile app are synced with the web version.

    ✦ Once an event ends, the event will no longer appear on the "*Saved*" events page (on both the web-based version and the mobile app).

OR:

1. Go to an event detail page for an event.

2. Once inside the event detail page, click the *bookmark icon* 🔖 (upper right corner).

To view a previously saved event:

✦ Click the *"Me"* button 👤 (bottom menu bar).

✦ Swipe your phone screen to the left to view *"Saved"* events.

✦ Click on the event listing to view the event detail page.

Screenshot 8-20   *Screenshot 8-21*

Screenshot 8-22   Screenshot 8-23

To save an event on the Eventbrite app, click the bookmark icon in the lower right corner of each event listing (Screenshot 8-20). Change the bookmark icon from white to orange (Screenshot 8-21). Save an event inside an event detail page by clicking the same bookmark icon in the upper right corner (Screenshot 8-22 & 8-23).

Screenshot 8-24

Screenshot 8-25

Screenshot 8-26

Click the "Me" button (bottom menu bar; Screenshot 8-24), and swipe your phone screen to the left to view your "Saved" events (Screenshot 8-25). Click an event listing to view the event detail page for a saved event (Screenshot 8-26).

Idea #178: Understand How to Register or Get Tickets for an Event with the Eventbrite App

1. Locate and click on a previously saved event to see the detail page for the event (See Idea #177).

2. Click the green *"Register"* or *"Get Tickets"* button.

3. Select the *type* of tickets you want to order.

4. Select *how many* tickets you want to order.

5. Verify your order and click *"Continue."*

6. Select *"Complete order."*

7. *"Order complete"* will now appear on your screen.

The ticket (QR Code) for the event can be found in *"Tickets"* once the order is complete.

Screenshot 8-27

Screenshot 8-28

Screenshot 8-29

Screenshot 8-30

Screenshot 8-31   Screenshot 8-32

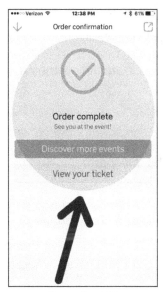

Screenshot 8-33

To register and get tickets for an event, click the "Register" button on an event detail page (Screenshot 8-27). Select the type of tickets you want to order or purchase (Screenshot 8-28). Select the quantity of tickets (Screenshot 8-29), and select "Done" (Screenshot 8-30). Verify the order and click "Continue" (Screenshot 8-31). Next, click "Complete order" (Screenshot 8-32) and the screen will say "Order complete" (Screenshot 8-33).

Idea #179: Understand How to Find out Which Facebook Friends Are Attending an Eventbrite Event

Before RSVP'ing or Purchasing Tickets to an Event:

▲ Go to any event detail page on the Eventbrite app.

▲ Look for the Facebook logo, and click *"See Who's Going"* (center of the screen).

▲ A pop-up box will appear.

▲ Click *"Connect with Facebook"* on the pop-up box, and follow the prompts.

OR:

After RSVP'ing or Purchasing Tickets to an Event:

▲ Click the *"Me"* button 👤 (bottom menu bar).

▲ Swipe your phone screen, and locate *"Ticket"* view.

▲ Choose an event you have already registered or purchased tickets to attend.

- ▲ The ticket for the event will be displayed.
- ▲ Click the "Info" tab (top center of the screen).
- ▲ Select *"See who's going"* (center of the screen, above the date of the event).
- ▲ A pop-up box will appear.
- ▲ Click *"Connect with Facebook"* on the pop-up box, and follow the prompts.

Screenshot 8-34

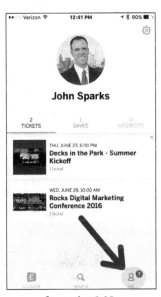

Screenshot 8-35

Screenshot 8-36

Screenshot 8-37

Screenshot 8-38

Screenshot 8-39

Screenshot 8-40

To see Facebook friends who are also attending an event, click "See Who's Going" on an event page you have not already RSVP'd to attend (Screenshot 8-34). For an event you have already purchased tickets or RSVP'd to attend, click the "Me" button (bottom menu bar; Screenshot 8-35). Next, swipe to the "Tickets" view (Screenshot 8-36), and locate the event (Screenshot 8-37). Click on the event, and view the event ticket. Click the "Info" tab at the top of the event ticket (Screenshot 8-38). Click "See who's going" (Screenshot 8-39). A pop-up box will appear. Click "Connect with Facebook" on the pop-up box, and follow the prompts. (Screenshot 8-40).

Idea #180: Understand How to Share Your Ticket to a Previously Ordered Event inside the Eventbrite App

▲ Click the *"Me"* button 🧍 (bottom menu bar).

▲ Change views, if necessary, and locate *"Ticket"* view.

▲ Click on the event you wish to share.

▲ The ticket for the event will be displayed.

▲ Click the *share icon* (↗ (right corner of the screen).

▲ Share your ticket via:

✦ Email

✦ Facebook Messenger

✦ Google +

✦ Google Drive

✦ LinkedIn

✦ Pinterest

✦ Evernote

✦ Post it in your Apple Notes

Screenshot 8-41

Screenshot 8-42

Screenshot 8-43

To share your Eventbrite ticket from the Eventbrite app, click the "Me" button. Next, locate the ticket in "Tickets" view (Screenshot 8-41). Open the ticket and click the share icon (upper right corner; Screenshot 8-42). After, choose how you want to share the ticket (Screenshot 8-43).

Idea #181: Add Events for Tickets to Your Calendar Using the Eventbrite App

▲ Click the *"Me"* button 🙎 (bottom menu bar).

▲ Swipe the phone screen and make sure you are in *"Ticket"* view.

▲ Choose the event you want to add to your iPhone or Android calendar.

▲ The ticket for the event will be displayed.

▲ Select *"Add to My Calendar."*

▲ Make any necessary edits to the event.

▲ Click *"Add"* and put the event on your calendar.

Screenshot 8-44

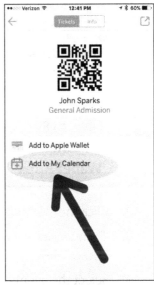

Screenshot 8-45

Screenshot 8-46

To add an event you've RSVP'd to attend to your calendar, click the "Me" button and locate the ticket in "Tickets" view. (Screenshot 8-44). Open up the ticket and click "Add to My Calendar" (center, Screenshot 8-45). Make any necessary edits, and click "Add" (Screenshot 8-46).

Idea #182: Save Upcoming Tickets for Later Use in the Apple/Google Wallet Apps

1. Click the *"Me"* button **ᗺ** ᴍᴇ (bottom menu bar).

2. Change views (if needed), and locate *"Ticket"* view.

3. Select the event you want to add to your Apple or Google wallet.

4. The ticket for the event will be displayed.

5. Select *"Add to Apple Wallet,"* or *"Add to Google Wallet."*

6. Select *"Add"* (right corner of the screen) once the ticket appears on your phone.

7. Click on the Apple or Google Wallet app.

8. Present the QR Code to be scanned for entry at an event.

Screenshot 8-47

Screenshot 8-48

Screenshot 8-49

Screenshot 8-50

Screenshot 8-51

Click the "Me" button, and locate the "Tickets" view to find an event (Screenshot 8-47). Once you find the event, click the event to go inside of it and select "Add to Apple/Google Wallet" (Screenshot 8-48). An event ticket will appear which you can add to your Apple or Google Wallet app (Screenshot 8-49). Go inside your Apple or Google Wallet app (Screenshot 8-50) and you will see the Eventbrite ticket has been added (Screenshot 8-51).

Idea #183: Understand How to Use Your Ticket Inside Your Apple/Google Wallet

▲ Click ⓘ to view the reverse side of the event ticket inside your Apple or Google wallet (bottom right corner of the screen).

✦ Click *"Open"* to open the event ticket, and access more features inside the Eventbrite app (upper right corner of the screen).

✦ Click *"Share Pass"* to share the ticket on social media.

✦ Delete your ticket from the wallet (See Idea #185).

▲ Click **E** to open the Eventbrite app and access more features (lower left corner of the screen).

From the event ticket inside the Eventbrite app:

▲ Share your ticket with other users on social media.

▲ Add the event to the calendar.

▲ Click the *"Info"* tab to:

✦ Get a description of the event.

✦ *"See Who's Going"* on Facebook.

✦ Use GPS and Apple Maps to locate or get directions to the event.

Screenshot 8-52

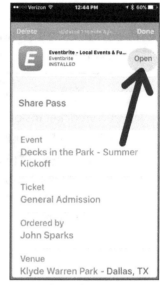

Screenshot 8-53

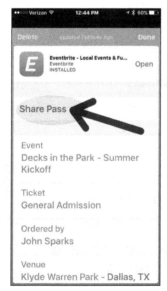

Screenshot 8-54

Screenshot 8-55

On an Eventbrite ticket inside the Apple/Google Wallet, click "i" to view the reverse side of a ticket (Screenshot 8-52). On the reverse side of a ticket, click "Open" to open the event ticket inside of the Eventbrite app and access more features (upper right corner of the screen; Screenshot 8-53). Click "Share Pass," to share the ticket on social media (Screenshot 8-54). Click "E" to open the Eventbrite app and access more features (lower left corner of the screen; Screenshot 8-55).

Idea #184: Understand How to Return to Your Apple/Google Wallet after Viewing Your Ticket in the Eventbrite App

To get back to your Apple or Google Wallet after viewing the ticket inside the Eventbrite app:

▲ Select *"Back to wallet"* (upper left corner of the Eventbrite ticket).

✦ *"Back to wallet"* will only appear when a ticket is accessed using the Apple or Google Wallet.

Screenshot 8-56

To get back to your Apple or Google Wallet, after viewing the ticket inside the Eventbrite app, select "Back to wallet."

 ## Idea #185: Understand How to Delete an Eventbrite Ticket from Your Apple/Google Wallet

1. Click 🛈 to view the reverse side of your event ticket inside the Apple or Google wallet (bottom right corner).
2. Once you are viewing the reverse side of the ticket, click on *"Delete"* (upper left corner of the screen).

3. Verify you want to delete the ticket.

4. Deleting a ticket from the Apple or Google wallet does not cancel your RSVP.

5. Deleting a ticket only removes your ticket from your wallet app.

6. To cancel your RSVP, see Idea #186.

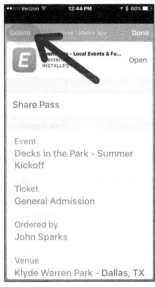

Screenshot 8-57   *Screenshot 8-58*

Screenshot 8-59

To delete an Eventbrite ticket from your "Wallet," click the "i" (bottom right corner; Screenshot 8-57). The details of the event will be displayed. Click on "Delete" (upper left corner; Screenshot 8-58). Next, a pop-up box will appear. Verify you want to delete the ticket (Screenshot 8-59). Remember, deleting a ticket from the Apple/Google Wallet does not cancel your RSVP. It only removes your ticket from your wallet app.

Idea #186: How to Cancel an Eventbrite RSVP

▲ Free events can *only* be canceled using the web-based version of Eventbrite.

▲ Free events *cannot* be canceled using the Eventbrite app.

✦ The fact that free events *cannot* be canceled from the Eventbrite app could lead to several serious problems:

● Users, who create their RSVP on the app, may forget or choose not to go through the trouble of changing their RSVP on the web-based version if they decide not to go to an event.

● Organizers, spending time and money planning for attendees, may end up disappointed when turn-out is not as expected.

▲ To cancel and request a refund for a paid event, "Contact The Organizer" using the web-based version of Eventbrite.

See Idea #171 for more on cancelling an RSVP using the web-based version of Eventbrite.

Idea #187: Know How to Adjust Email Notifications and Get To "Eventbrite Support" on the Eventbrite App

▲ Click the *"Me"* button ⚇ ᴍᴇ (bottom menu bar).

▲ Click the *settings icon* ⚙ (right corner of the screen).

   ✦ On the *"Settings"* page:

      • Click *"Push Notifications"* to adjust the following email notifications:

         ✧ *"Announcements"*

         ✧ *"Friend updates"*

      • Select *"Help"* to access Eventbrite support.

Screenshot 8-60

Screenshot 8-61

Screenshot 8-62

Screenshot 8-63

Screenshot 8-64

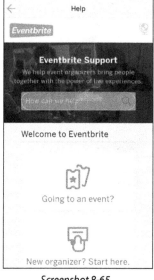

Screenshot 8-65

To adjust email notifications on the Eventbrite app, click the "Me" button (bottom menu bar; Screenshot 8-60) and then click the settings icon (Screenshot 8-61). To change push notifications, select "Push Notifications" (Screenshot 8-62). Adjust the push notifications for "Announcements" and "Friend updates" (Screenshot 8-63). To get to the "Eventbrite Support" page, select "Help," from the "Settings" page (Screenshot 8-64). The "Eventbrite Support" page will appear (Screenshot 8-65).

PART 9
Have Fun Finding Events with Facebook

 Idea #188: Know Where to Go to Find Facebook Events

For those feeling like a social butterfly, consider trying out Facebook events.

▲ **Access Facebook events on the Facebook website at:**

http://www.Facebook.com

▲ **iPhone users can download the Facebook app by going to:**

https://itunes.apple.com/us/app/facebook/id284882215?mt=8

▲ **Android users can download the Facebook app by going to:**

https://play.google.com/store/apps/
details?id=com.facebook.katana&hl=en

Screenshot 9-1

Facebook app in the Apple iTunes Store.

 ## Idea #189: Decide If Facebook Is the Right Place to Post Your Event

▲ Facebook has an estimated 1.71 billion monthly active users and growing.

▲ Facebook is over six times the size of Meetup.com, which has 27.24 million users.

▲ Users create more events on Facebook, per half hour, than they do on Meetup.com in one month and Eventbrite.com in one year.

✦ Every half-hour 1,485,000 events are created on Facebook (Source: Bloggerwitts, February 2015).

✦ Meetup.com reports over 567-thousand monthly Meetups on their website (Source: Meetup.com, September 2016).

✦ Eventbrite reported 1.7 million events in 2014 (Source: Eventbrite, January 2015).

Because of the high user traffic on Facebook and the large quantity of Facebook users, the potential exists to have an event seen by a bigger audience. In fact, events can reach thousands of people within a very short period of time.

Facebook has made a lot of changes recently to Facebook events.

▲ To Facebook's credit, one of the best changes to happen lately is a change that allows Facebook users the ability to block other users from sending event invitations to you.

✦ The ability to block users from sending event invitations has helped to limit the mass quantity of events being sent out by marketers.

✦ The number of SPAM invites on Facebook continues to decline.

✦ The quality of the types of events you will find on Facebook has steadily improved.

 ## Idea #190: Know What Kinds of Events You Are Likely to Find on Facebook

Facebook users can create events for almost anything imaginable.

▲ Facebook users can create either one-time events or events that reoccur, like the ones found on Meetup and Eventbrite.

▲ Facebook events tend to appeal to the masses.

▲ Facebook events can be either small or large social gatherings.

▲ Because of Facebook's large number of users, it is not unusual to see hundreds of people getting invited to some Facebook events.

▲ Sometimes several organizers will pull their resources together on Facebook and will send out invites to the masses.

Idea #191: Understand Why It's Important to Know the Five Basic Categories of Facebook Events

Why is it important to know the five different categories of Facebook events?

- ▲ The category of an event will determine where the event will appear on Facebook and how visible the event is.
    - ✦ Visibility of the event could have an impact on:
        - The number of users who respond to the event invitation.
        - Turnout at the event.

 ## Idea #192: Know the Five Basic Categories of Facebook Events

Facebook events can fall into one or several of 5 categories:

1. Events You Are Invited To
    - ✦ Friends on Facebook have invited you to attend these events.
    - ✦ Appear in "Upcoming" 🗓️ events under the *"All"* tab and the *"Invites"* tab.

- Options for how users respond to these events will depend on whether the event is a(n):
  - ✧ Public event
  - ✧ Private event
  - ✧ Event popular in your network

2. Suggested events
   - ✦ Facebook friends have not personally invited you to attend these events. Facebook is suggesting these events to you based on places you've checked into, pages you like, and events your friends say they're going to attend.
   - ✦ Appear in *"Upcoming"* 📅, *"Subscribed"* 📶, and *"Past"* 🕐 events pages.
     - Options for responding to suggested events include:
       - ✧ *"Interested"*
         - ◆ You might or might not choose to attend the event.
         - ◆ After selecting *"Interested,"* a suggested event will appear as an *"Upcoming"* event.

- ✦ *"Going"*

    - ♦ You are going to attend the event.

    - ♦ After selecting "Going," a suggested event will appear as an *"Upcoming"* event.

  - • Examples of suggested events include:

    - ✦ Events happening this week

    - ✦ Popular with friends

    - ✦ Related events

    - ✦ Suggested for you

    - ✦ Events Near (Your City)

3. Subscribed events

  - ✦ Users elect to receive notice about these events by going to a Facebook fan page and then subscribing to see them.

    - • Similar to suggested events, options for responding to subscribed events include:

      - ✦ *"Interested"*

      - ✦ *"Going"*

    - • Examples include local tour dates for a popular musician, actor, etc.

4. Public events

   ✦ Both users, who have a Facebook account and those who don't, can see the descriptions, wall posts, photos, and videos related to these events.

   • Options for responding to public events include:

      ✧ *"Interested"*

      ✧ *"Going"*

      ✧ *"Ignore"*

   • Options for responding to public events that are also suggested events or subscribed events include:

      ✧ *"Interested"*

      ✧ *"Going"*

      ✧ *"Not interested"* (only after *"Interested"* has been selected)

      ✧ *"Not Going"* (only after *"Going"* has been selected)

   • Organizers of public events receive notifications when people say they are *"Interested"* or *"Not Going."*

5. Private events

   ✦ Facebook events that are only visible to users who are invited to attend.

- Options for users responding to private events include:
  - ✧ *"Going"*
  - ✧ *"Not Going"*
  - ✧ *"Maybe"*
- Only users who receive invitations to these events are able to view details about the events.
- Organizers can choose whether or not to allow invitees to send out invitation requests to these events.
- Organizers and guests can see who's viewed an event invitation.

 ### Idea #193: Understand How to Tell If a Facebook Event Is an Event You've Personally Been Invited to Attend or Is a Suggested Event

You can tell if an event is one you've personally been invited to attend, or is one Facebook is suggesting you attend, by looking at where the event appears on Facebook.

See Idea #192 to find out where the events you've personally been invited to attend and the suggested events are displayed.

Idea #194: Know How to Get to the Event Pages and Listings on Facebook

To get to the event pages and listings on Facebook:

▲ Click *"Home"* (top blue nav menu).

▲ Click on *"Events"* (left-hand side menu, under the section that says *"Favorites"*).

▲ Facebook events menu will appear. By default, the *"Upcoming"* 📅 event listings are displayed on the screen.

▲ The options on the Facebook events menu, called *"My Events,"* include:

✦ *"Upcoming"* 📅

✦ *"Calendar"* 🗔

✦ *"Discover"* 🧭

✦ *"Subscribed"* 📶

✦ *"Past"* 🕒

✦ *"Create"* 📆

Screenshot 9-2

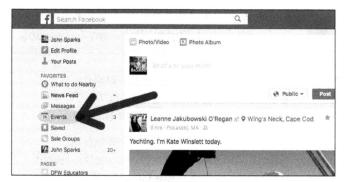

Screenshot 9-3

Screenshot 9-4

To get to the Facebook event listings, click "Home" (top blue nav menu; Screenshot 9-2). Select "Events" (left side nav menu, under "Favorites"; Screenshot 9-3). The "Upcoming" event listings will appear. To view the other event listings, select "Calendar," "Discover," "Subscribed," "Past," or "Create" on the Facebook events menu, called "My Events" (Screenshot 9-4).

Idea #195: Understand How to Get to an Event Detail Page on Facebook

▲ Follow the steps in Idea #194 and go to the Facebook events menu (*"My Events"*)/*"Upcoming"* events pages.

▲ Click any event on the event listings in "Upcoming" events or any of the other event pages you are interested in seeing.

▲ The Facebook event detail page for the event will be displayed.

 Idea #196: Understand The Anatomy of a Facebook Event Detail Page

▲ The Facebook event detail page includes:

✦ Name of the event

✦ Dates

✦ Location

✦ Type of the event

• Public

• Private

✦ Name of the person who sent the invitation

✦ RSVP Options

✦ # of people

- • Interested

- • Going

- • Invited

✦ Event details

✦ Links to Related Events

✦ Place to invite friends

✦ Event discussion board

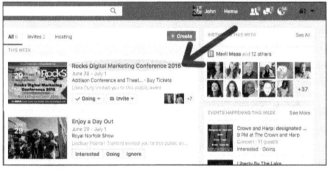

Screenshot 9-5

Screenshot 9-6

To view a Facebook event detail page, click on any event on the "Upcoming" event listings page you're interested in seeing (Screenshot 9-5). The Facebook event detail page for the event will be displayed (Screenshot 9-6).

Idea #197: Know How to Find the Events Others Are Inviting You to Attend on Facebook and Determine If the Events Are Public Events or Private Events

▲ Follow the steps in Idea #194 and go to the Facebook events menu ("*My Events*")/"*Upcoming*" [20] events pages.

▲ Click on either the "All" tab or the "Invites" tab (top center of the page, under the top blue nav menu).

  ✦ A list of events you've received invitations for but haven't responded to will appear in the top section of both tabs.

  ✦ The name of the user who's inviting you or sharing the event with you will appear underneath the event location.

    • "Public event" or "Private event" will appear after the name of the person inviting you so you'll know if the event is a public event or a private event.

✧ See Idea #192 for more details
on the features of "Public
Events" and "Private Events."

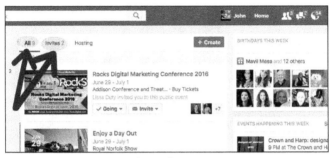

Screenshot 9-7

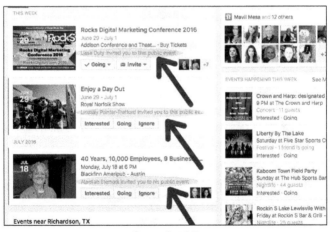

Screenshot 9-8

*To view the name of the user who sent a Facebook invitation,
go to "Upcoming" events and click on either the "All" tab or the
"Invites" tab (top of the screen, under the top blue nav menu;
Screenshot 9-7). The name of the user who's inviting you or
sharing the event with you will appear under the location of the
event (Screenshot 9-8).*

Idea #198: Learn How to View Facebook Events You Are Hosting

▲ Follow the steps in Idea #194 and go to the Facebook events menu (*"My Events"*)/*"Upcoming"* 20 events pages.

▲ Click on the *"Hosting"* tab (top center of the page, to the right of the "Invites" tab).

  ✦ If you're organizing or hosting an upcoming event, the event will appear here.

  ✦ If you're not organizing or hosting any events, you will see the option to create a new event.

Screenshot 9-9

A list of upcoming events you're organizing or hosting will appear under the "Hosting" tab in "Upcoming" events. If you're not organizing or hosting any upcoming event, you will see the option to create a new event.

Idea #199: Know How to Remove an Event From "Upcoming" Events That You Have Received an Invitation to

To remove an event you've received an invitation to attend from *"Upcoming"* events:

▲ Follow the steps in Idea #194 and go to the Facebook events menu (*"My Events"*)/*"Upcoming"* 20 events pages.

▲ Hover over the event you want to remove.

▲ A pop-up ✖ will appear (upper right corner of each event listing, to the right of each event name).

▲ Hover over the pop-up ✖.

▲ A small pop-up box will appear that says *"Remove event."*

▲ Click the pop-up ✖ to remove the event.

▲ The event is removed from the *"Upcoming"* event listings.

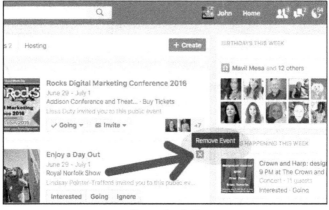

Screenshot 9-10

Hover over the pop-up "X" on an event and click the "X" to remove the event from your "Upcoming" events (upper right corner of each event listing, to the right of each event name).

 ## Idea #200: Understand How to Block Facebook Users from Sending You Event Invitations

▲ Follow the steps in Idea #199 to remove an event from *"Upcoming"* 📅 events.

▲ After removing the event, a notification will appear on your *"Upcoming"* events page that says *"You removed this event."*

▲ On this same notification, you will be given the option to *"Stop Invites from (the sender)"* or *"Dismiss"* the notification.

✦ Select *"Stop Invites from (the sender)"*
  and a pop-up box will appear.

  ● Choose "OK" on the pop-up box
    to confirm you want to block all
    invites from the sender.

  ● A second notification will appear
    on the *"Upcoming"* events page
    that says *"You blocked invitations
    from (the sender)."*

  ● Invites from the Facebook user
    will no longer appear in your
    "Upcoming" events.

✦ Select *"Dismiss"* and you will continue
  to receive invites from the Facebook
  user.

  ● The notification you received
    which says that the event has been
    removed from your *"Upcoming"*
    events will also disappear.

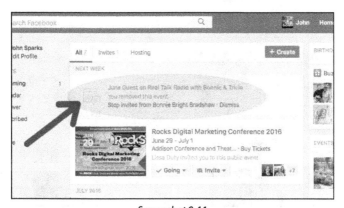

Screenshot 9-11

Screenshot 9-12

Screenshot 9-13

Screenshot 9-14

To block Facebook users from sending you event invitations, follow the steps in Idea #199 to remove an event from "Upcoming" events. After removing the event, a notification will appear on your "Upcoming" events page that says "You removed this event" (Screenshot 9-11). On this same notification, you will be given the option to "Stop Invites from (the sender)" or "Dismiss" the notification. Select "Stop Invites from (the sender)" (Screenshot 9-12) and a pop-up box will appear (Screenshot 9-13). Choose "OK" on the pop-up box to confirm you want to block all invites from the sender. A second notification will appear on the "Upcoming" events page that says "You blocked invitations from (the sender)" (Screenshot 9-14). Invites from the user will no longer appear in your "Upcoming" events.

Idea #201: Understand Another Way to Block Facebook Users from Sending You Event Invitations

1. Click the upside-down triangle (top right of the screen, on the top blue nav menu) on any Facebook page.

2. Select *"Settings"* from the drop-down menu that appears.

3. Click *"Blocking"* (left-hand side menu, in the second section).

4. Scroll down the *"Manage Blocking"* page and locate the section that says *"Block event invites."*

5. In the box that says *"Block Invites from,"* type in the user's name you want to block from sending you invitations.

You will no longer receive event invitations from the user. (See Screenshots 9-15 through 9-19 for a step-by-step illustration of this process).

 Idea #202: Understand How to Unblock Facebook Users from Sending You Event Invitations

1. Click the upside-down triangle (top right of the screen, on the top blue nav menu) on any Facebook page.

2. Select *"Settings"* from the drop-down menu that appears.

3. Click *"Blocking"* (left-hand side menu, in the second section).

4. Scroll down the *"Manage Blocking"* page and locate the section that says *"Block event invites."*

5. Locate a user's name on the list of blocked users and click *"Unblock"* after their name.

You will now be able to receive event invitations from the user.

Screenshot 9-15

Screenshot 9-16

Screenshot 9-17

Screenshot 9-18

Screenshot 9-19

To either block or unblock a user from sending you event invites on Facebook, click the upside-down triangle (top right of the screen, on the top blue nav menu) on any Facebook page

(Screenshot 9-15). Select "Settings" from the drop-down menu that appears (Screenshot 9-16). Click on "Blocking" (left-hand side menu, in the second section; Screenshot 9-17). Scroll down the "Manage Blocking" page and locate the section that says "Block event invites" (Screenshot 9-18). To block a user from sending you invites, type in the user's name in the box that says "Block Invites from" (Screenshot 9-19). To unblock a user, locate a user's name on the list of blocked users and click "Unblock" after their name (Also see Screenshot 9-19).

 ## Idea #203: Know Where Suggested Events Appear on Facebook

Suggested events are events that Facebook friends have not personally invited you to attend. Facebook is suggesting these events to you based on places you've checked into, pages you like, and events your friends say they're going to attend.

Even though Facebook friends have not personally invited you to attend these events, you can still select that you're "*Interested*" in these events or that you're "*Going*" to these events.

Suggested events appear under the following five section headings:

- ▲ Events Near (Your City)
- ▲ Popular with Friends
- ▲ Suggested for You
- ▲ Events Happening This Week
- ▲ Related Events

1. **Events Near (Your City):**

   ▲ Events that appear in this section are near your current location or are determined by GPS location tracking on your phone app.

   ▲ To view the listing of *"Events Near (Your City)"*:

   ✦ Follow the steps in Idea #194 and go to the Facebook events menu (*"My Events"*)/*"Upcoming"* 20 events pages.

   ✦ In *"Upcoming"* events, click on either the *"All"* tab or the *"Invites"* tab (top center of the page, under the top blue nav menu).

      • Scroll down to the second section on the page (below the section which has the events that you've been invited to) and look for the section heading that says *"Events Near (Your City)."*

      • Two boxes will appear under the heading.

      • Inside one of the boxes you will see the words, *"Today (See More)."* Inside the other box you will see the words, *"This Weekend (See More)."*

   ✦ Click the *right arrow* ❯ located to the right of *"Today (See More)"* or *"This Weekend (See More)"* to filter the suggested events by when they are taking place.

OR:

▲ Follow the steps in Idea #194 and go to the Facebook events menu (*"My Events"*)/*"Upcoming"* 📅 events pages.

▲ Click *"Discover"* ⊘ (located on the Facebook events menu, under *"My Events"* on the left-hand side of the page).

  ✦ *"Events Near (Your City)"* will appear.

  ✦ See Idea #209 for more on how to *"Discover"* ⊘ events on Facebook.

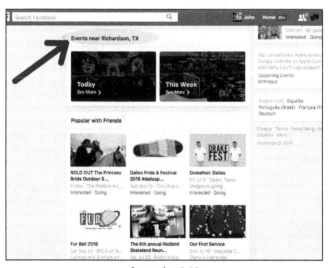

Screenshot 9-20

To view "Events Near (Your City)," follow the steps in Idea #194 and go to the Facebook events menu ("My Events")/"Upcoming" events pages. In "Upcoming" events, click on either the "All" tab or the "Invites" tab (top center of the page, under the top blue nav menu). Scroll down to the second section on the page (below the section which has the events that you've been invited to) and look for the section heading that says "Events Near (Your City)." Two boxes will appear under the heading. Inside one of the boxes you will see the words "Today (See More)." Inside the other box you will see the words "This Weekend (See More)." Click the right arrow located to the right of "Today (See More)" or "This Weekend (See More)" to filter the suggested events by when they are taking place.

2. ***Popular with Friends:***

▲ Events that appear in this section are the events your Facebook friends say they're going to attend.

▲ To view a listing of suggested events that are "*Popular with Friends*":

✦ Follow the steps in Idea #194 and go to the Facebook events menu ("*My Events*")/"*Upcoming*" 📅 events pages.

✦ In "*Upcoming*" events, click on either the "*All*" tab or the "*Invites*" tab (top center of the page, under the top blue nav menu).

✦ Scroll down to the third section on the page.

✦ Below the section heading that says "*Popular with Friends*" you will find a listing of events your Facebook friends say they're going to attend.

- Select either ★ Interested or + Going on the event listing for one of these events or inside the event detail page.

- The event will now appear in your "*Upcoming*" events.

- Click the *down arrow* ∨ on the event picture of a "*Popular with Friends*" event listing and select:

  ✧ "*Show me a new suggestion*"

    ♦ The event will disappear and a new one will take its place.

  ✧ "*Report the event*"

    ♦ A pop-up box will appear and you can report the event to Facebook for:

      - Harassment
      - Sexually explicit material
      - Spam or scam
      - Violence or harmful behavior
      - Hate speech
      - Unauthorized use of intellectual property

Screenshot 9-21

To view events that are "Popular with Friends," follow the steps in Idea #194 and go to the Facebook events menu ("My Events")/"Upcoming" events pages. In "Upcoming" events, click on either the "All" tab or the "Invites" tab (top center of the page, under the top blue nav menu). Scroll down to the third section on the page and locate the section heading that says "Popular with Friends" and you will find a listing of events your Facebook friends say they're going to attend."

3. **Suggested for You:**

▲ Your Facebook activity and online search history will determine the events that appear here.

▲ To view the listing of events that are "*Suggested for You*":

✦ Follow the steps in Idea #194 and go to the Facebook events menu ("*My Events*")/"*Upcoming*" 🗓 events pages.

✦ In "*Upcoming*" events, click on either the "*All*" tab or the "*Invites*" tab (top center of the page, under the top blue nav menu).

✦ Scroll down to the fourth section on the page.

✦ Below the section heading that says "*Suggested for You*" you will find a listing of events related to your Facebook activity and online search history.

   • Click the *down arrow* ⌄ on an event picture of a "*Suggested for You*" event listing and select:

      ✧ "Show me a new suggestion"

      ✧ "Report the event"

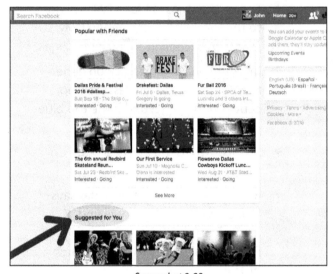

Screenshot 9-22

To view events that are "Suggested for You," follow the steps in Idea #194 and go to the Facebook events menu ("My Events")/"Upcoming" events pages. In "Upcoming" events, click on either the "All" tab or the "Invites" tab (top center of the page, under the top blue nav menu). Scroll down to the fourth section on the page. Below the section heading that says "Suggested for You" you will find a listing of events related to your Facebook activity and online search history.

4. **Events Happening This Week:**

   ▲ Like the name implies, suggested events found in this section are happening this week.

      ✦ To view a listing of *"Events Happening This Week"*:

- Follow the steps in Idea #194 and go to the Facebook events menu ("*My Events*")/"*Upcoming*" 🗓️ events pages.

- On the "*Upcoming*" events page, you will find "*Events Happening This Week*" on the right side of the page (underneath "*Birthdays This Week*").

✦ "*Events Happening This Week*" can also be found on the "Subscribed" or "Past" events pages:

- Follow the steps in Idea #194 and go to the Facebook events menu ("*My Events*")/"*Upcoming*" 🗓️ events pages.

- Click "*Subscribed*" 🔖 or "*Past*" 🕓 (located on the Facebook events menu under "*My Events*" on the left-hand side of the page).

- You will also find "*Events Happening This Week*" on the right side of both the "*Subscribed*" and the "*Past*" events pages.

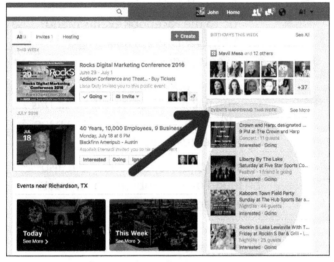

Screenshot 9-23

"Events Happening This Week" appear on the right side of the page on the "Upcoming," "Subscribed," and "Past" events pages.

5. **Related Events:**

▲ To see events similar to event listings you're looking at, follow the steps in Idea #195 to view a Facebook event detail page for an event.

▲ Scroll down the event detail page and look on the right side of the page.

▲ *"Related events"* (event listings for other events that are similar to the one you're looking at) will appear in a box underneath the section that allows you to "Invite Friends" to the event.

Screenshot 9-24

Screenshot 9-25

To get to "Related events," follow the steps in Idea #195 to view a Facebook event detail page for an event. Scroll down the event detail page and look on the right side of the page (Screenshot 9-24). "Related events" (event listings for other events that are similar to the one you're looking at) will appear in a box underneath the section that allows you to "Invite Friends" to the event (Screenshot 9-25).

Idea #204: View a Calendar of "Upcoming" Events You've Been Invited to and Your Friends' Birthdays

▲ Follow the steps in Idea #194 and go to the Facebook events menu (*"My Events"*)/*"Upcoming"* 📅 events pages.

▲ Click *"Calendar"* 🗒 (located on the Facebook events menu under *"My Events"* on the left-hand side of the page).

✦ A calendar showing all your events will appear.

• Events you have been invited to and have RSVP'd to will appear as blue links.

• Events you've been invited to but have not yet RSVP'd to will appear as gray links.

• Pictures and names of Facebook friends celebrating birthdays will appear underneath these events.

✧ Hover the cursor over a friend's picture who's celebrating a birthday and their name will be displayed.

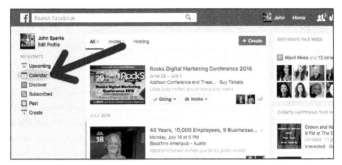

Screenshot 9-26

Screenshot 9-27

Screenshot 9-28

To view a calendar of "Upcoming" events you've been invited to and your friends' birthdays, follow the steps in Idea #194 and go to the Facebook events menu ("My Events")/"Upcoming" events pages. Click "Calendar" (located on the Facebook events menu under "My Events" on the left-hand side of the page; Screenshot 9-26). At the top of each calendar date, events you have been invited to will appear first (Screenshot 9-27). Below the events are pictures and names of friends celebrating birthdays (Screenshot 9-28).

Idea #205: Know a Quick Way to View a List of Your Event Invites and the Upcoming Events on the Calendar You're Going to Attend

To view a list of your event invites and the upcoming events on the calendar you're going to attend:

▲ Click *"Home"* (top blue nav menu).

　　✦ Your Facebook News Feed will be displayed.

▲ Look for the *"Upcoming" icon* 20 on the right-hand side of the page (above birthdays).

▲ Click either "*[Number] event invites*" or the title of an event you are going to attend.

▲ If you click on "*[Number] event invites,*" a pop-up box will appear allowing you to:

　　✦ See a list of events you've been invited to attend.

✦ Click on the title of an event and go to the event detail page.

✦ Respond to the event by selecting: "*Interested*," "*Going*," "*Ignore*" (Public events) or by selecting: "*Going*," "*Maybe*," "*Can't Go*" (Private events).

✦ Click a link to view all "Upcoming" 📅 events.

✦ Create an event.

▲ If you click on the title of an event you have already said you're going to attend, a pop-up box appears allowing you to:

✦ Change your response to the event by selecting: "*Interested*," "*Going*," "*Ignore*" (Public events) or by selecting: "*Going*," "*Maybe*," "*Can't Go*" (Private events).

✦ Invite others to the event.

✦ Click a link to view all "Upcoming" 📅 events.

✦ Create an event.

Screenshot 9-29

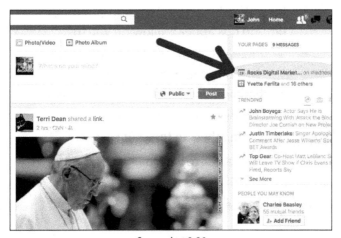

Screenshot 9-30

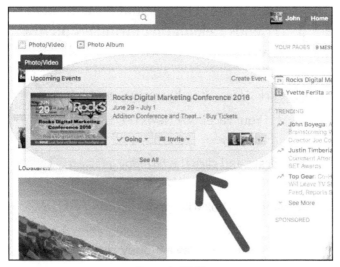

Screenshot 9-31

For a quick way to view events you're going to attend, click "Home" (top blue nav menu) and your Facebook News Feed will be displayed (Screenshot 9-29). Look for the "Upcoming" events icon on the right-hand side of the page (above birthdays). Select the title of the next upcoming event (Screenshot 9-30). A pop-up box will appear. In the pop-up box: change your response to the event, invite others to the events, click a link to view all "Upcoming" events, or create a new event (Screenshot 9-31).

Idea #206: Understand How to View Friends Celebrating Birthdays on Any given Date

▲ Click *"Home"* (top blue nav menu).

   ✦ Your Facebook News Feed will be displayed.

▲ Locate and click the *birthday gift* icon 🎁 (underneath the *"Upcoming" icon*).

▲ A pop-up box will appear allowing you to:

   ✦ Wish friends that are celebrating a birthday today a "Happy Birthday."

   ✦ Select *"Upcoming Birthdays"* to view previous and upcoming birthdays.

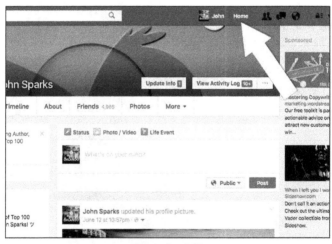

Screenshot 9-32

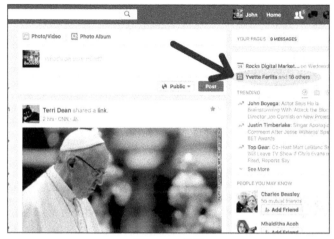

Screenshot 9-33

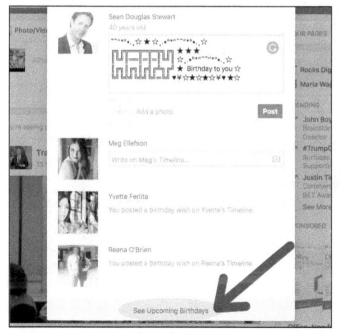

Screenshot 9-34

To view friends celebrating birthdays on any given date, click "Home" and return to the Facebook News Feed (Screenshot 9-32). Look to the right of the Facebook News Feed for the birthday gift icon (underneath the "Upcoming" events icon; Screenshot 9-33). Click the birthday gift icon. A pop-up box will appear allowing you to post a birthday wish on your friends' timeline. Scroll to the bottom of the pop-up box and select "See Upcoming Birthdays" to view birthdays that are taking place today, yesterday, later this week, and later this month (Screenshot 9-34).

Idea #207: Understand How to Export Upcoming Events and Birthdays to Your Calendar

1. Click *"Home"* (top blue nav menu).

2. Click on *"Events"* (left-hand side menu).

3. The *"Upcoming"* [20] event listings appear.

    ✦ Scroll down the page.

    ✦ Look for a small box on the right side of the page (under *"Events Happening This Week"*) to add your events to Microsoft Outlook, Google Calendar, or Apple Calendar.

4. Click at the bottom of the box where it says *"Upcoming Events"* or *"Birthdays"* to export all your upcoming events or birthdays.

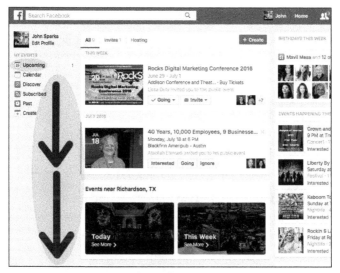

Screenshot 9-35

Screenshot 9-36

To export upcoming events and birthdays to your calendar, go to "Upcoming" events and scroll down the page (Screenshot 9-35). Look for a small box on the right side of the page (under

"Events Happening This Week") to add your events to Microsoft Outlook, Google Calendar, or Apple Calendar (Screenshot 9-36). Click at the bottom of the box where it says "Upcoming Events" or "Birthdays" to export all your upcoming events or birthdays.

Idea #208: Understand How to Export Individual Events to Your Google or iCal Calendars

1. Follow the steps in Idea #195 and go to a Facebook event detail page for an event you've been invited to attend and wish to export.

2. Click the menu button represented by three dots ⌐···⌐ (located underneath the right corner of the event header graphic and to the right of the box that says "*Invite*").

3. Select "*Export Event*" (from the drop-down menu).

   ✦ A pop-up box will appear.

4. Select the options to "*Save to calendar,*" "*Send to email,*" or click the link provided to subscribe to all upcoming events on your calendar.

   ✦ Users are only able to export events that they have been invited to attend.

   ✦ Users cannot export suggested events.

Screenshot 9-37

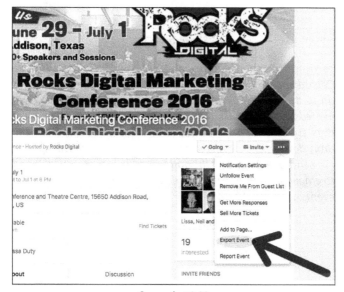

Screenshot 9-38

Screenshot 9-39

To export an individual event to Microsoft Outlook, Google Calendar, or Apple Calendar, follow the steps in Idea #195 and go to a Facebook event detail page for an event you've been invited to attend. Click the "More" button represented by three dots (Screenshot 9-37). Next, select "Export event" from the drop-down menu (Screenshot 9-38). A pop-up box will appear. (Screenshot 9-39). Select the options to "Save to calendar," "Send to email," or click the link provided to subscribe to all upcoming events on your calendar.

Idea #209: Understand How to Use "Discover" on Facebook

▲ Follow the steps in Idea #194 and go to the Facebook events menu ("*My Events*")/"*Upcoming*" 20 events pages.

▲ Click "*Discover*" ⊘ (located on the Facebook events menu under "*My Events*" on the left-hand side of the page).

   ✦ "*Events Near (Your City)*" will appear.

▲ Use the menu on the left side of the page to filter the events by time:

   ✦ All

   ✦ Today

   ✦ Tomorrow

   ✦ This week

   ✦ This weekend

   ✦ Next week

   ✦ Choose a date

▲ On this same menu, select to filter events by location:

   ✦ Near your city

   ✦ In your city

   ✦ In a city nearby

✦ Select "⋯ More" to choose a different
   city that you type in (bottom of the
   list).

▲ Select the category to search (located to
   the right side of the event listings):

   ✦ Music

   ✦ Nightlife

   ✦ Food/Drinks

   ✦ Sports/Fitness

   ✦ Fine Arts/Crafts

   ✦ Film/Photography

   ✦ Performing Arts

   ✦ Community

   ✦ Causes

   ✦ Other

▲ Click the [★ Interested] button on any of these
   events.

▲ The [★ Interested] button will change to
   [✓ Interested ▾].

▲ The event will now appear on the
   "*Upcoming*" events page.

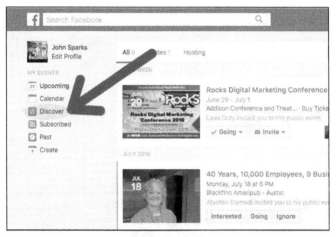

Screenshot 9-40

Screenshot 9-41

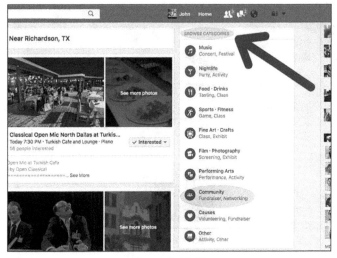

Screenshot 9-42

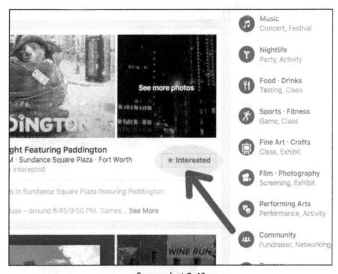

Screenshot 9-43

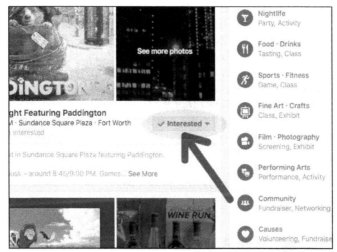

Screenshot 9-44

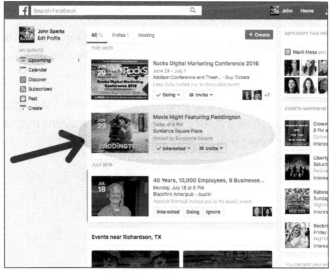

Screenshot 9-45

To "Discover" events on Facebook by time, location, and category follow the steps in Idea #194 and go to the Facebook events menu ("My Events")/"Upcoming" events pages. Click "Discover" (located on the Facebook events menu under "My Events" on the left-hand side of the page; Screenshot 9-40). Use the menu on the left side of the page to filter the events by time and location (Screenshot 9-41). Next, select the category to search (Screenshot 9-42). A new listing of events will appear. Click "Interested" on any event you are interested in (Screenshot 9-43). The icon on the "Interested" button will change from a star to a checkmark (Screenshot 9-44). The event will now appear in your "Upcoming" events (Screenshot 9-45).

Idea #210: Understand the Benefit of Using Subscribed Events on Facebook

Are you interested in keeping up with the performance schedules and touring dates of your favorite actors, singers, musicians, or performers?

When you subscribe to events for a Facebook fan page, you will receive a notice on your Facebook event pages when an event will be happening near you.

Idea #211: Understand How to Subscribe to Events on Facebook

To subscribe and receive notices about events related to a Facebook fan page:

▲ Find the Facebook fan page for a popular actor, singer, musician, or performer.

▲ Click the 🔊 Subscribe button on the Facebook fan page (underneath the right corner of the header graphic).

▲ The 🔊 Subscribe button will change to ✓ Subscribed

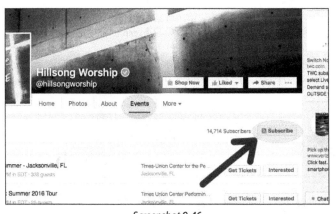

Screenshot 9-46

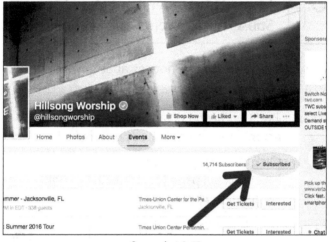

Screenshot 9-47

To subscribe to a Facebook fan page, find the fan page for a popular actor, singer, musician, or performer that you want to receive notices about. Click the "Subscribe" button on the page (underneath the right corner of the header graphic; Screenshot 9-46). The "Subscribe" button will change to "Subscribed" (Screenshot 9-47).

Idea #212: Understand How to View Subscribed Events on Facebook

▲ Follow the steps in Idea #194 and go to the Facebook events menu ("*My Events*")/"*Upcoming*" 📅 events pages.

▲ Click "*Subscribed*" 🔊 (located on the Facebook events menu under "*My Events*" on the left-hand side of the page).

▲ Select the *"Subscribed"* tab (top center of the page, under the top blue nav menu).

▲ If the fan page you are subscribed to has any events scheduled for your area, they will appear here.

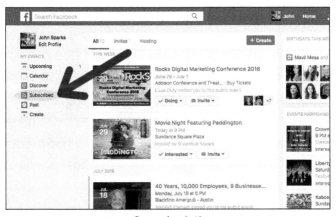

Screenshot 9-48

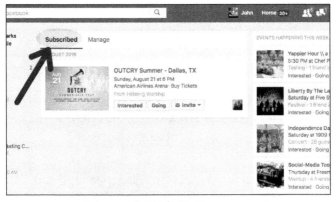

Screenshot 9-49

To view "Subscribed" events, follow the steps in Idea #194 and go to the Facebook events menu ("My Events")/"Upcoming" events pages. Click "Subscribed" (located on the Facebook events menu under "My Events" on the left-hand side of the page; Screenshot 9-48). Click the "Subscribed" tab (top center of the page, under the top blue nav menu; Screenshot 9-49). If the fan page you are subscribed to has any events scheduled for your area, they will appear here.

Idea #213: Understand How to Stop Receiving Notifications about Subscribed Events on Facebook

To stop receiving notifications about subscribed events on Facebook:

1. Click *"Home"* (top blue nav menu).

2. Click *"Events"* (left-hand side menu).

3. Click on *"Subscribed"* (located on the Facebook events menu under *"My Events"* on the left-hand side of the page).

4. Select the "Manage" tab (top center of the page, under the top blue nav menu).

5. Click the ⟨ ✓ Subscribed ⟩ button under the picture of the actor, singer, musician, or performer you want to stop receiving notifications from.

6. The ⟨ 🔊 Subscribe ⟩ button will appear and you will stop receiving notifications from the artist about events near you.

If you decide you made a mistake and want to re-subscribe to a page, make sure to do so before leaving the "Manage" page. Once you leave this page, you'll have to go back to the Facebook fan page if you want to subscribe again.

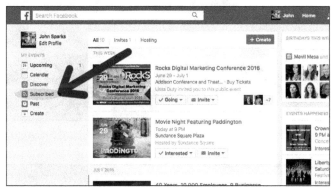

Screenshot 9-50

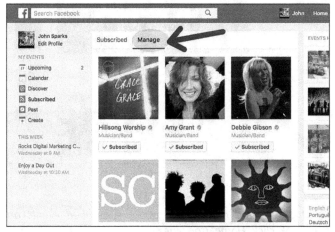

Screenshot 9-51

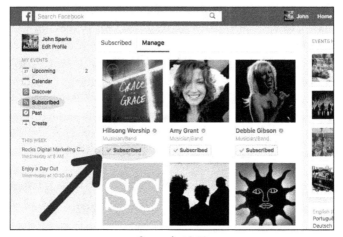

Screenshot 9-52

Screenshot 9-53

To stop receiving notifications about subscribed events on Facebook, click "Home" (top blue nav menu), "Events" (left-hand side menu), and then "Subscribed" (located on the Facebook *events menu under "My Events" on the left-hand side of the page; Screenshot 9-50). Select the "Manage" tab (top center of the page, under the top blue nav menu; Screenshot 9-51). Click the "Subscribed" button under the picture of the actor, singer, musician, or performer you want to stop receiving notifications from (Screenshot 9-52). The "Subscribe" button will appear and you will stop receiving notifications from the artist about events near you (Screenshot 9-53).*

 ## Idea #214: Understand What You Will Find on The "Past" Events Page on Facebook

▲ On the "Past" events page you will find:

  ✦ A listing of all past events you have been invited by others to attend.

  ✦ *"Recent Birthdays."*

  ✦ Suggested *"Events Happening This Week."*

 ## Idea #215: Know How to View Past Events on Facebook

▲ Click *"Home"* (top blue nav menu).

▲ Select *"Events"* (left-hand side menu).

▲ Choose *"Past"* 🕘 (located on the Facebook events menu under *"My Events"* on the left-hand side of the page).

"*Past*" Events appear in descending chronological order with the most recent events you've been invited to appearing at the top of the page.

"*Recent Birthdays*" appear to the right of the past event listings in the top box. "*Events Happening This Week*" are located underneath "*Recent Birthdays*."

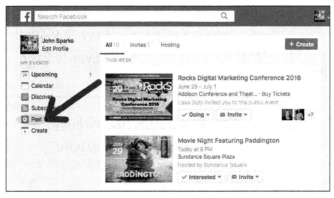

Screenshot 9-54

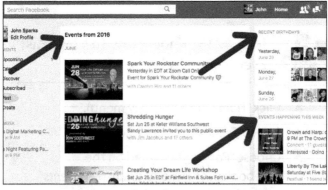

Screenshot 9-55

To view past events on Facebook, click "Home" (top blue nav menu), "Events" (left-hand side menu), and then "Past" (located on the Facebook events menu under "My Events" on the left-hand side of the page; Screenshot 9-54). You will find past events, that you have been invited to, sorted by month and year in descending chronological order. Also on the page, you will find "Recent Birthdays" and "Events Happening This Week" (Screenshot 9-55).

Idea #216: How to View Events Right after They Are Created with Facebook Notifications

▲ Click the *"Globe" icon* (top blue nav menu).

▲ A drop-down menu will appear.

▲ All of your Facebook notifications can be found in this drop-down menu in descending chronological order.

▲ Notifications of events will also appear here after they are created and posted on Facebook.

▲ Click the notification for any event you've received and go to the Facebook event detail page for the event.

Screenshot 9-56

Notifications for Facebook events appear by clicking the "Globe" icon on any Facebook page. Notifications appear in the drop-down after the events are created and posted on Facebook.

 ### Idea #217: Know How to Turn off Notifications for an Event through a Facebook Event Detail Page

▲ Click the notification for any event you've received or follow the steps in Idea #195 and go to a Facebook event detail page.

▲ Click the *"More"* button ⋯ represented by three dots on the Facebook event detail page (underneath the Facebook event header image, on the right-hand side of the page).

▲ Select *"Notification Settings"* from the drop-down menu.

▲   A pop-up box will appear on your screen.

▲   Choose to receive "*All Notifications*," "*Highlights*" (important notifications about the event), "*Host Updates Only*" (any time a host posts in the event), *or turn all notifications:* "*Off.*"

 ## Idea #218: View RSVP'ing to Facebook Events in Real-Time

Keep up with all your friends as they RSVP to Facebook events.

▲   Monitor your Facebook ticker/live feed (far right side of any Facebook page) when you're logged into the web-based version of Facebook.

▲   The Facebook ticker will show you when a friend responds to a Facebook event in real-time.

To check out and respond to an event a friend is responding to:

1.   Hover over the event update in the Facebook ticker/live feed

2.   A pop-up box will appear with:

    ✦   The name of the event.

    ✦   The date of the event.

    ✦   The location of the event.

✦ How long ago your Facebook friend said they were "*Interested*" or "*Going*" to the event.

✦ Icons that will allow you to like, comment, or share the event with others.

3. Click the ★ Interested button while hovering over the event update to express interest in the event.

4. Once you express interest, the event will appear in your "*Upcoming*" events.

Screenshot 9-57

Facebook events are displayed in real-time on the Facebook ticker.

Idea #219: Know How to Invite Facebook Friends of Your Choice to Attend a Public Event Through a Facebook Event Detail Page

▲ Click the ☒ Invite ▾ button on a Facebook event detail page.

   ✦ The ☒ Invite ▾ button is underneath the Facebook event page graphic on the right-hand side.

▲ Select *"Choose Friends"* from the drop-down menu.

▲ Select friends to invite from:

   ✦ Suggested friends

   ✦ All friends

   ✦ Close friends

   ✦ Friends in your area

   ✦ Family events hosted

   ✦ Events attended

   ✦ Groups

To select friends:

1. Click anywhere in the box with the friend's name on it.

   ✦ A checkmark will appear to the right of the friend you select.

2. Click *"Send Invites."*

Screenshot 9-58

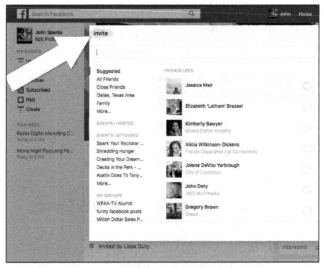

Screenshot 9-59

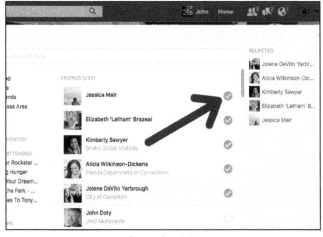

Screenshot 9-60

To invite friends of your choice to attend a Facebook event, click the "Invite" button on the Facebook event detail page for the event you want to invite them to (Screenshot 9-58). Select "Choose Friends" from the drop-down menu. Next, a pop-up box will appear to "Invite" friends (Screenshot 9-59). Find and select the friends you want to invite and click "Send invites" (Screenshot 9-60).

Idea #220: Understand How to Share a Public Facebook Event on Your Facebook Page

▲ Click the ⌈ ✉ Invite ▾ ⌉ button on the Facebook event detail page of any public event.

▲ Select *"Share Event"* from the drop-down menu.

▲ A pop-up box will appear with the event inside of it that you selected.

✦ Add a comment to the event before sharing it if you choose.

• Choose where you want to share the event:

✧ On your timeline

✧ On a friend's timeline

✧ In a group

✧ On a page you manage

✧ In a phone message

• Select who you want to see the event:

✧ Make it available to the public on your timeline

✧ Make it available only to friends

✧ Make it available to only yourself

▲ Click the "*Post*" button (lower right corner of the pop-up box) to share the event.

Screenshot 9-61

Screenshot 9-62

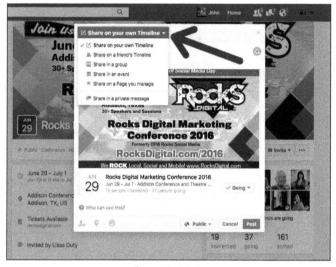

Screenshot 9-63

Screenshot 9-64

To share an event, go to an event you've been invited to attend. Click the "Invite" button and select "Share Event" from the drop-down menu (Screenshot 9-61). A pop-up box will appear with the event inside of it that you selected (Screenshot 9-62). Choose where you want to share the event (Screenshot 9-63) and who you want to see the event (Screenshot 9-64). Click the "Post" button (lower right corner of the pop-up box) to share the event.

Idea #221: Understand How to Create an Event on Facebook

1. Click "*Home*" (top blue nav menu).

2. Select "*Events*" (left-hand side menu).

3. Choose "*Create*" 🔳 (located on the Facebook events menu under "*My Events*" on the left-hand side of the page).

4. A pop-up box will appear on your screen.

5. Choose to make the event a "*Public Event*" or a "*Private Event*" by clicking the `⊠ Create Private Event ▾` button (upper left-hand corner of the pop-up box).

6. Enter the details of the event you want to schedule.

7. Click "*Create*" (lower right corner of the pop-up box) to create the event.

Another way to create an event is by choosing "*Upcoming*" 🔳 or "*Calendar*" 🔳 on the Facebook events menu under "*My Events.*"

If selecting "*Upcoming*," click + Create (to the right of the "*All*" tab and the "*Invites*" tab). The same pop-up box will appear allowing you to enter the details of the event.

If selecting "*Calendar*" ⬜ , hover over the date on the calendar that you want to create your event. Click the word "*Create*," which will appear in the upper right-hand corner of the calendar box for the date you're selecting.

Screenshot 9-65

Screenshot 9-66

There are several ways to "Create" an event on Facebook. One way is to click "Create" under "My Events" on the Facebook events menu (Screenshot 9-65). After clicking "Create," a pop-up box will appear allowing you to enter the details of the event you want to schedule. Another way is to either click "Upcoming" events or "Calendar" under "My Events" on the Facebook events menu. If selecting "Calendar," hover over the date on the calendar that you want to create your event and then click on the word "Create." (Screenshot 9-66).

Idea #222: Getting More Help with Facebook Events

When it comes to Facebook events, we've only just begun to get started. There's so much more you can do with Facebook events.

For more info on Facebook events, check out the Facebook Help Center: https://www.facebook.com/help/?helpref=facebar_dropdown_help

OR:

▲ Click the upside-down arrow (located on the top blue nav menu).

▲ A drop-down menu will appear.

▲ Select *"Help."* The shortcut "Help Center" menu will appear.

▲ Enter the topic to search for in the shortcut "Help Center," or select "Visit the Help Center" (bottom of the short-cut "Help Center" menu) to visit Facebook's "Help Center" page.

Screenshot 9-67

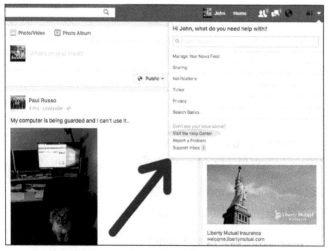

Screenshot 9-68

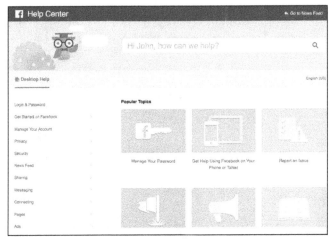

Screenshot 9-69

For more help with Facebook events, visit the Facebook Help Center. Click the upside-down triangle (located on the top blue nav menu; Screenshot 9-67). Select "Help" from the drop-down menu. The shortcut "Help Center" menu will appear. Select "Visit the Help Center" (bottom of the short-cut "Help Center" menu; Screenshot 9-68) to visit Facebook's "Help Center" page (Screenshot 9-69).

Other helpful Facebook links include:

Creating and Editing Events
https://www.facebook.com/help/131325477007622/

Viewing and Responding to Events
https://www.facebook.com/help/25719794396580/

Sharing and Promoting Events
https://www.facebook.com/help/656156637816003/

Event Tagging
https://www.facebook.com/help/264693833649910/

Events Privacy
https://www.facebook.com/help/216355421820757/

Birthdays and Celebrations
https://www.facebook.com/help/422017727841283/

PART 10

Thumbs up to Events on the Facebook App

 Idea #223: Finding All Upcoming Facebook Events on the Facebook App

Facebook events can also be found on the Facebook App—and they're easier to navigate, too!

To locate Facebook events on the Facebook app:

1. Click *"More"* ≡ (bottom menu bar).
2. Select *"Events"* on the Facebook app menu listing.
3. You will see a listing of all *"Upcoming"* 🗓 Facebook events (See Idea #192 for a list of the types of events included here).

4. Click any event to see the Facebook event detail page.

5. From the Facebook event detail page you can:

   ✦ Select *"Going"* ⌄⌄ Going to indicate you're attending the event.

   ✦ Click the *"Share"* ⤴ Share or *"Invite"* ✉ Invite button to:

     • Choose friends from a list to share the event with (*"Choose friends …"*).

     • Share the event in a post (*"Share Event in a Post"*).

     • Share the event in Facebook Messenger (*"Share Event in Messenger"*).

     • Share the event on another social media site through your phone (*"More Sharing Options …"*).

   ✦ Click the *"More"* button ⋯ More with three dots to:

     • Save the event (*"Save"*).

     • Copy the link and share the event link on other social media sites (*"Copy link"*).

     • Change the event notifications for the event (*"Notification Settings"*).

     • Report the event to be reviewed by Facebook (*"Report event"*).

Screenshot 10-1

Screenshot 10-2

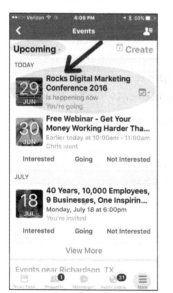

Screenshot 10-3

Screenshot 10-4

To find all upcoming Facebook events on the Facebook app, click "More" (bottom menu bar; Screenshot 10-1). Select "Events" on the Facebook app menu listing to navigate to the "Upcoming" events page (Screenshot 10-2). All "Upcoming" Facebook events will appear (Screenshot 10-3). Click any event to see the Facebook event detail page for that event (Screenshot 10-4). Select "Going" to indicate you are going to the event. Click "Share" or "Invite" to share the event. Click the "More" button to access a menu with more functions, which include saving the event.

Idea #224: Find Facebook Events You've Received Invitations to Attend on the Facebook App

1. Click *"More"* ☰ (bottom menu bar).

2. Click *"Events"* on the Facebook app menu listing.

3. Click the upside-down triangle, located to the right of the page heading that says *"Upcoming,"* (top, upper left of the screen) to reveal the Facebook events menu.

4. Select *"Invites"* ✉ on the Facebook events menu.

5. A listing of Facebook events you've received invites to and haven't responded to will appear.

Screenshot 10-5

Screenshot 10-6

Screenshot 10-7

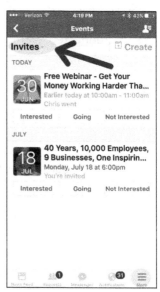

Screenshot 10-8

To find events you've received invitations to attend on the Facebook app, click "More" (bottom menu bar) and then click "Events" on the Facebook app menu listing (Screenshot 10-5). Next, click the upside-down triangle located to the right of "Upcoming" to reveal the Facebook events menu (Screenshot 10-6). Select "Invites" on the Facebook events menu (Screenshot 10-7). A listing of Facebook events you've received invites to and haven't responded to will appear (Screenshot 10-8).

 ## Idea #225: Find Suggested Events on the Facebook App

To find suggested events on the Facebook app:

1. Follow steps #1-3 in Idea #223 and locate your "*Upcoming*" events.

2. Scroll down the "*Upcoming*" events page.

3. Suggested events will appear right after the "*Upcoming*" events.

The section headings for the suggested events include:

✦ "*Events Near (Your City)*"

✦ "*Popular with Friends*"

✦ "*Suggested for You*"

✦ "*Categories*"

Screenshot 10-9

Screenshot 10-10

Screenshot 10-11

Screenshot 10-12

To view suggested events using the Facebook app, follow steps #1-3 in Idea #223 and locate your "Upcoming" events. (Screenshot 10-9). Scroll down the "Upcoming" events page (Screenshot 10-10). Suggested events will appear right after the "Upcoming" events, under the section headings: "Events Near (Your City)," "Popular with Friends" (Screenshot 10-11), "Suggested for You," and "Categories" (Screenshot 10-12).

 ## Idea #226: Understand How to Find Events by Category on the Facebook App

To locate events by category on the Facebook app:

1. Follow steps #1-3 in Idea #223 and locate your "*Upcoming*" events.

2. Scroll down the "*Upcoming*" events page.

3. Locate the section heading that says "*Categories.*"

4. Click on one of the categories *(Music, Nightlife, Food/Drinks, etc.).*

5. Swipe your phone screen to the left to filter events by when they are taking place *(All, Today, Tomorrow, This Weekend, etc.).*

6. Click the upside-down triangle (top center of the screen, under the name of the category) to select the location you want to view events for *(Near your city, In your city, In a city nearby, etc.).*

7. To change categories, click the button that says "*[Number] Filter*" (upper right corner of the screen).

8. After finding an event that you're interested in, select either "*Interested*" or "*Going.*" on the event detail page.

9. The event will now appear in your "*Upcoming*" events.

Screenshot 10-13

Screenshot 10-14

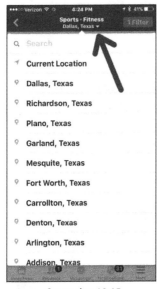

Screenshot 10-15

Screenshot 10-16

Screenshot 10-17

To locate events by category on the Facebook app, follow steps #1-3 in Idea #223 and locate your "Upcoming" events. Scroll down the "Upcoming" events page and locate the section heading that says "Categories." Select a category (Screenshot 10-13) and event listings for that category will be displayed. Swipe your phone screen to the left to filter events by when they are taking place (Screenshot 10-14). Click the upside-down triangle (top center of the screen, under the name of the category) to select the location you want to view events for (Screenshot 10-15). To change categories, click the button that says "[Number] Filter" (upper right corner of the screen; Screenshot 10-16). After selecting a different category of interest (Screenshot 10-17), find the event you are interested in and select "Interested" or "Going." The event will now appear in your "Upcoming" events.

Idea #227: Access Birthdays and Send Birthday Greetings Using the Facebook App

To access birthdays and send birthday greetings using the Facebook app:

▲ Follow steps #1-3 in Idea #223 and locate your "*Upcoming*" events.

▲ Scroll down to the bottom of the page and click the right arrow ❯ next to the section heading that says "*Upcoming Birthdays.*"

▲ A list of everyone celebrating a birthday (today, tomorrow, later this week, etc.) will appear.

▲ Click the *post icon* ☑ (located to the right of a person's name).

▲ A new page will appear to post your birthday greeting. Click anywhere in the message box (top of the page) and compose your birthday greeting.

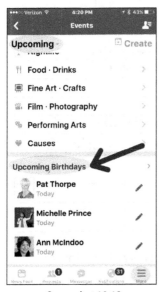

Screenshot 10-18

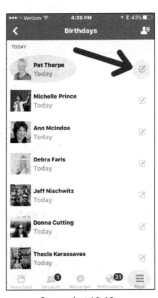

Screenshot 10-19

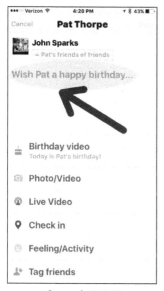

Screenshot 10-20   *Screenshot 10-21*

To access birthdays and send birthday greetings using the Facebook app, follow steps #1-3 in Idea #223 and locate your "Upcoming" events. Scroll down to the bottom of the page and click the right arrow next to the section heading that says "Upcoming Birthdays." (Screenshot 10-18). A list of everyone celebrating a birthday (today, tomorrow, later this week, etc.) will appear. Click the post icon (located to the right of a person's name; Screenshot 10-19). A new page will appear to post your birthday greeting (Screenshot 10-20). Click anywhere in the message box (top of the page) and compose your birthday greeting (Screenshot 10-21).

Idea #228: Learn How to View Events You Are Hosting and Create New Events through the Facebook App

To view events you are hosting:

1. Click *"More"* ☰ (bottom menu bar).
       More

2. Select *"Events"* on the Facebook app menu listing.

3. Click the upside-down triangle, located to the right of the page heading that says *"Upcoming,"* (top, upper left of the screen) to reveal the Facebook events menu.

4. Select *"Hosting"* 🏠 on the Facebook events menu.

5. If you're hosting any *"Upcoming"* events, they will appear here.

To create an event from the "Hosting" page:

1. Follow steps #1-4 above and go to the *"Hosting"* page.

2. Click *"Create"* ⊞ (upper right corner of the *"Hosting"* page).

3. On the *"Create Event"* page, click the upside-down triangle (top center of the screen) to change the event from private to public.

4. Enter the event title.

5. Click the picture icon 🖼 (located to the right of the event title) and upload a photo or choose a theme for the event.

6. Select the time and location of the event, enter a description (under *"More info"*), and choose whether or not guests may invite friends.

7. Select *"Co-hosts"* and choose friends to co-host the event with you.

8. Click the word *"Create"* (upper right corner of the *"Create Event"* page) to post the event on Facebook.

In addition to the *"Hosting"* page, events can be created by selecting any of these other pages on the Facebook events menu:

▲ *"Upcoming"*

▲ *"Invites"*

▲ *"Past"*

▲ *"Saved"*

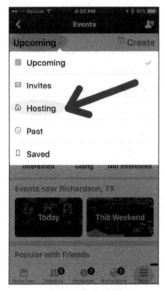

Screenshot 10-22

Screenshot 10-23

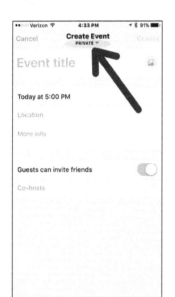

Screenshot 10-24

Screenshot 10-25

Screenshot 10-26

Screenshot 10-27

Screenshot 10-28

Screenshot 10-29

To view events you are hosting, click "More" (bottom menu bar) and then select "Events" on the Facebook app menu listing. Next, click the upside-down triangle located to the right of the page heading: "Upcoming" to reveal the Facebook events menu. Select "Hosting" (Screenshot 10-22). If you're hosting any "Upcoming" events, they will appear here. To create an event from the "Hosting" page, click "Create" (upper right corner of the page; Screenshot 10-23). On the "Create Event" page, click the upside-down triangle (top center of the screen; Screenshot 10-24) to change the event from private to public (Screenshot 10-25). Click the picture icon (located to the right of the event title; Screenshot 10-26) and upload a photo or choose a theme for the event (Screenshot 10-27). After entering the event details, select "Co-hosts" (Screenshot 10-28) and choose friends to co-host the event with you (Screenshot 10-29). Click "Create" (upper right corner of the "Create Event" page) to post the event on Facebook.

Idea #229: Know How to View Past Events on the Facebook App

▲ Click "*More*" ≡ (bottom menu bar).

▲ Select "*Events*" on the Facebook app menu listing.

▲ Click the upside-down triangle, located to the right of the page heading that says "*Upcoming*," (top, upper left of the screen) to reveal the Facebook events menu.

▲ Select "*Past*" 🕐 on the Facebook events menu.

▲ Past events will appear in descending
  chronological order.

   ✦ The most recent events you have been
     invited to appear at the top of the
     page.

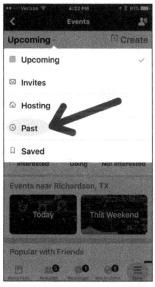

Screenshot 10-30   Screenshot 10-31

*To view past events on the Facebook app, click "More" (bottom
menu bar) and then select "Events" on the Facebook app menu
listing. Next, click the upside-down triangle located to the right
of the page heading: "Upcoming" to reveal the Facebook events
menu. Select "Past" (Screenshot 10-30). Past events will appear
on the screen in descending chronological order (Screenshot
10-31). The most recent past event will appear at the top of the
page.*

Idea #230: Understand How to Save and Retrieve an Event Using the Facebook App

To save a Facebook event to return to it later:

▲ Go to the Facebook event detail page for the event you want to save.

▲ Click the "*More*" button ⋯ **More** with three dots to access a pop-up menu with more features.

▲ A pop-up menu will appear (bottom of the screen).

▲ Select "*Save.*"

+ Only events that Facebook friends have not personally invited you to attend can be saved.

+ Once saved, events will appear on the "*Upcoming*" events page.

To retrieve a previously saved event:

▲ Click "*More*" ≡ **More** (bottom menu bar).

▲ Select "*Events*" on the Facebook app menu listing.

▲ Click the upside-down triangle, located to the right of the page heading that says "*Upcoming*" (top, upper left of the screen) to reveal the Facebook events menu.

▲ Select *"Saved"* 🔖 on the Facebook events menu.

▲ Saved events will be displayed in chronological order.

Screenshot 10-32

Screenshot 10-33

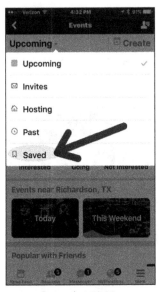

Screenshot 10-34   *Screenshot 10-35*

Screenshot 10-36

To save an event, go to the Facebook event detail page for the event you want to save. Click the "More" button with three dots to access a pop-up menu with more features (Screenshot 10-32). Select "Save" on the pop-up menu (Screenshot 10-33). The event will appear on the "Upcoming" events page (Screenshot 10-34). You can retrieve "Saved" events by going to the events menu and clicking "Saved." (Screenshot 10-35). A list of all the saved events will appear in chronological order (Screenshot 10-36).

 ### Idea #231: Getting More Help on Facebook Events on the Mobile App

▲ Click *"More"* ☰ (bottom menu bar).

▲ Scroll down the page.

▲ Click *"Help and Support."*

▲ A pop-up menu will appear (bottom of the screen).

▲ Select *"Help Center."*

▲ The Facebook Help Center will appear.

▲ Enter a topic in the main search box to get help.

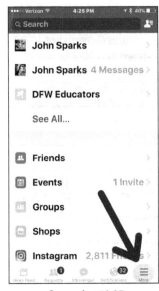

Screenshot 10-37

Screenshot 10-38

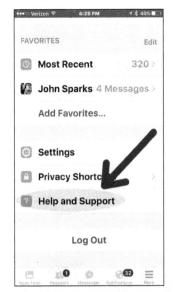

Screenshot 10-39

Screenshot 10-40

Screenshot 10-41

Click on "More" to navigate to the Facebook Help Center on the Facebook app (Screenshot 10-37). Scroll down the page (Screenshot 10-38). Locate and click "Help and Support" (Screenshot 10-39). A pop-up menu will appear. Select "Help Center" (bottom of the screen; Screenshot 10-40). The Facebook Help Center is displayed (Screenshot 10-41). Enter a topic in the main search box to get help.

PART 11
Become Awesome Using Yelp Events

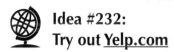
Idea #232:
Try out Yelp.com

Many people think of Yelp as primarily a place to read restaurant reviews. They don't realize Yelp has great event listings too!

There are so many terrific event listings on Yelp that your head will be spinning with delight trying to sort them all out.

▲ **Access Yelp through the web at:**

http://www.Yelp.com

▲ **iPhone users can download the Yelp app by going to:**

https://itunes.apple.com/us/app/yelp/id284910350?mt=8

▲ **Android users can download the Yelp app by going to:**

https://play.google.com/store/apps/
details?id=com.yelp.android&hl=en

Screenshot 11-1

Yelp app in the Apple iTunes Store

Idea #233: Understand Yelp Lingo for Yelp Events

Before getting started with Yelp events, it helps to understand some basic Yelp lingo:

- ▲ **CM (Community Manager):**
    - ✦ A paid position working for Yelp.
    - ✦ Each CM has a designated region, territory, or city.
    - ✦ Makes phone calls to set up events during the day.
    - ✦ Attends Yelp events at night.

- ▲ **CMYE (Community Manager Yelp Event):**
    - ✦ Type of an event on Yelp that is a small-scale event.
    - ✦ Planned and organized by the CM.
    - ✦ Typically held at area businesses.

- ▲ **Elites:**
    - ✦ Members of an exclusive group called the "Yelp Elite Squad."
    - ✦ Get invited to special events called "Yelp Elite Events."
    - ✦ Must be 21 years of age (or over the legal drinking age).

✦ You can nominate yourself or someone else by completing the form at http://www.yelp.com/elite

▲ **"*Events*" page:**

✦ The page on Yelp where a city's events are listed.

▲ **Event Spotlight:**

✦ Featured Yelp event.

▲ **"I'm In!":**

✦ One of 2 RSVP options on a Yelp event detail page.

✦ Button that is selected to indicate you are going to an event.

▲ **My Upcoming Events:**

✦ A section on the Yelp "*Events*" page (upper right side of the page) that shows events you have responded to.

✦ Events show up here after you select "*I'm In!*" (Going) or "*Sounds Cool*" (Maybe).

▲ **Official Yelp Event:**

✦ A type of event that is listed under the "*Official Yelp Events*" and the "*Popular Events*" section of the Yelp "*Events*" page.

✦ Events include Community Manager Yelp Events (CMYE), Yelper Parties, and Yelp Elite Events.

▲ **"Sounds Cool":**

✦ One of 2 RSVP options.

✦ Button that is selected to indicate you might attend an event.

▲ **UYE (Unofficial Yelp Event):**

✦ A type of event that is listed under the *"Popular Events"* or the *"Popular Events in [City Name]"* section of the Yelp *"Events"* page.

✦ UYE's are planned by Yelpers.

✦ The CM helps with promoting these events.

▲ **Weekly Yelp:**

✦ A weekly newsletter that features *"Popular Events This Week"* along with clips from Yelper reviews.

▲ **Yelp Elite Squad:**

✦ An exclusive group of "the most influential tastemakers" on Yelp.

✦ Members of this group are called "Elites."

- ▲ **Yelp Elite Event:**
    - ✦ A type of event that only members of Yelp's Elite Squad can attend.
    - ✦ Cannot be viewed publicly on the site and are only accessible to Elites.

- ▲ **"Yelper":**
    - ✦ Another term for a Yelp member.

- ▲ **Yelper Party:**
    - ✦ A type of an event on Yelp that is a large-scale private event.
    - ✦ Organized by several vendors.
    - ✦ Held once or twice a year.
    - ✦ Open to the entire Yelp community.

 Idea #234: Understand the Ups and Downs of Events on Yelp.com

Ups:

- ▲ Members say Yelp events are fun to go to and are fun networking opportunities.
- ▲ No Yelp account is needed to browse events.
- ▲ The web-based version of Yelp allows you to view, RSVP, and comment on events taking place in other cities.

Downs:

- ▲ Less populated cities don't have many event listings.

- ▲ You must have a Yelp account and be signed into the account to RSVP for an event.

- ▲ The Yelp app requires you to be in the same city that you are surfing events for, RSVP'ing for, and commenting on.

- ▲ The purpose of selecting the RSVP options "*I'm In!*" and "*Sounds Cool*" could sound vague and confusing to some. Because they might not be clear on when to select these options, some members may select them without ever having the intention of going to an event.

- ▲ Events are known to swell to capacity very quickly and have large wait lists.

- ▲ Members planning to attend Yelp events could change their mind about going to an event without notifying anyone. Others might be unable to sign up and this could mean low turnout at events.

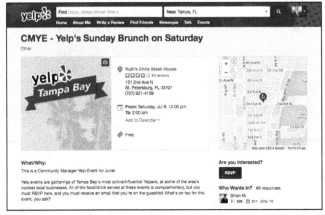

Screenshot 11-2

Example a of Community Manager Yelp Event ("CMYE" Event).

Idea #235: Read the Yelp Event Terms and Conditions and Yelp Elite Squad Terms of Membership Before RSVP'ing for an Event

Before attending your first Yelp event, make sure you read and understand the Yelp Event Terms and Conditions at http://www.yelp.com/static?p=event_tos

Members of Yelp's Elite Squad also need to read and understand these additional terms of membership at https://www.yelp.com/tos/elite_en_us_20120425

Idea #236: Understand How to View a Yelp "Events" Page for Another City

1. Click on *"Events"* (top of the screen, inside the top red nav menu) to select the city you want to view events for.

2. A listing of cities will appear (upper right of the screen, under the top red nav menu).

3. Select a city on the list or click *"More Cities"* (at the end of the list).

   a. If selecting *"More Cities"*, a new page listing of cities will appear.

      i. Choose either your home location, one of your *"Recently Used Locations,"* or a city from the list of *"Popular Cities."*

      ii. Click *"More Locations"* (bottom of the *"Popular Cities"* list) for a list of even more locations to choose from.

4. After choosing a city, the Yelp *"Events"* page for that city will appear.

5. Click any event to view the event detail page and RSVP for the event.

Screenshot 11-3

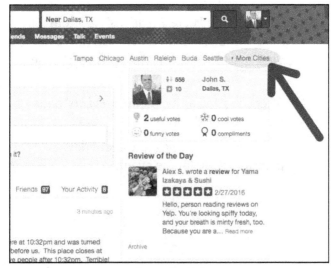

Screenshot 11-4

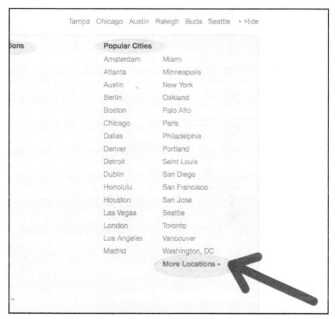

Screenshot 11-5

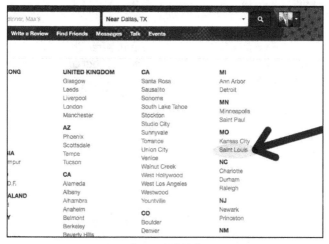

Screenshot 11-6

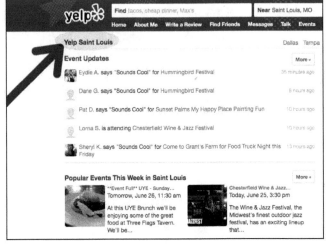

Screenshot 11-7

To go to a Yelp "Events" page for another city, click on "Events" (top of the screen inside the top red nav menu; Screenshot 11-3). A listing of cities will appear (upper right of the screen under the top red nav menu). Select a city on the list or click "More Cities" (at the end of the list; Screenshot 11-4). If selecting "More Cities", a new page listing of cities will appear. Click "More Locations" (bottom of the "Popular Cities," list; Screenshot 11-5) for a list of even more locations to choose from. After choosing a city (Screenshot 11-6), the Yelp "Events" page for that city will appear (Screenshot 11-7).

Idea #237: Understand Another Way to Get to a Yelp "Events" Page for Any City

1. Type the name of any city into the location search box (right box, top center of the page, inside the top red nav menu).

2. Click the *search icon* **Q** (right of the location search box) to start the search.

3. A listing of Yelp businesses for the new city will appear.

4. Click "Events" (top of the screen inside the top red nav menu) to view the Yelp "Events" page for that city.

5. Click any event to view the event detail page and RSVP for the event.

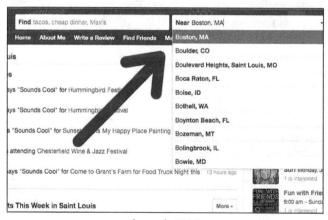

Screenshot 11-8

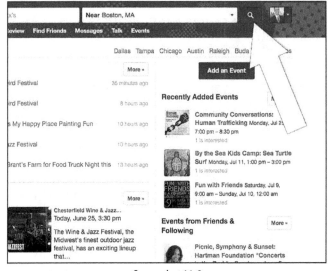

Screenshot 11-9

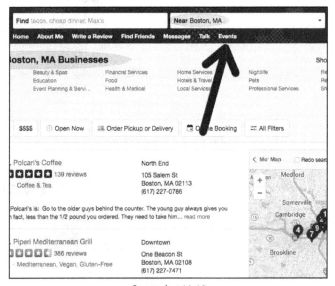

Screenshot 11-10

Screenshot 11-11

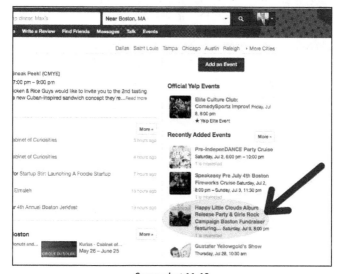

Screenshot 11-12

Screenshot 11-13

To go to a Yelp "Events" page for any city, type the name of any city into the location search box (right box, top center of the page, inside the top red nav menu; Screenshot 11-8). Click the search icon (right of the location search box) to start the search (Screenshot 11-9). A listing of Yelp businesses for the new city will appear. Click "Events" (top of the screen, inside the top red nav menu; Screenshot 11-10) to view the Yelp "Events" page for that city (Screenshot 11-11). Click any event (Screenshot 11-12) to view the Yelp event detail page and RSVP for the event (Screenshot 11-13).

Idea #238: Get to Know the Anatomy of a Yelp "Events" Page

The Yelp "*Events*" page is a dashboard for all things about events in a city you are searching. On a Yelp "*Events*" page you will find:

- ▲ **Event spotlight**: featured event on Yelp.

- ▲ **"Add an event:"** button that allows you to add a new event on Yelp.

- ▲ **Event updates**: anytime a user RSVPs, expresses interest, or comments on an event, it shows up here along with their name.

- ▲ **Your upcoming events**: After replying to an event by saying "*I'm In!*" or "*Sounds Cool*" the event will show up in this section.

- ▲ **Official Yelp events**: events created by a local Yelp Community Manager, such as cocktails and gatherings.

Scroll down further on this page to see:

- ▲ **Popular Events This Week** (by city)
- ▲ **Other Popular Events**

From "*Other Popular Events*," you can select and view events for: "*Today*," "*Tomorrow*," "*This weekend*," "*This week*," "*Next week*," or "*Jump to date*" (choose a date on the calendar).

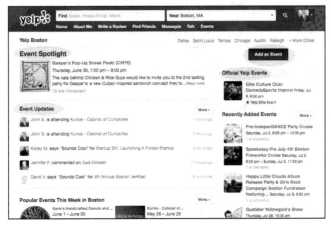

Screenshot 11-14

Screenshot 11-15

Screenshot 11-16

Screenshot 11-17

Features of a Yelp "Events" page include an event spotlight, event updates, Official Yelp Events, upcoming events you have RSVP'd to, and a button to click and "Add an Event" (Screenshot 11-14). To view other popular events in a city, scroll down to the bottom of the page and find the section heading that says "Other Popular Events" (Screenshot 11-15). Click to view other popular events for "Today," "Tomorrow," "This Weekend," "This Week," "Next week." When selecting "Jump to date" (Screenshot 11-16) a pop-up calendar will appear so you can select a date (Screenshot 11-17).

 Idea #239: Understand How to Do an Advanced Search for a Yelp Event

1. Follow the steps in Ideas #236-#237 to go to a Yelp *"Events"* page.

2. Click the *"More"* button (located towards the bottom of the page and to the right of *"Popular Events This Week in…"*).

3. On the left column of the next page you can choose to:

    ✦ Narrow events by time

    ✦ Sort events by:

       • Most Popular

       • Date

       • Recently Added

       • Friends & Following

       • Free

    ✦ Show events by category

    ✦ Show events intended for everybody or just the Yelp community.

Screenshot 11-18

Screenshot 11-19

To do an advanced search for a Yelp event, click the "More" button which is at the bottom of a Yelp "Events" page (Screenshot 11-18). On the left column of the next page you can choose to narrow events by time, sort events (most popular, date, recently added, etc.), show events by category, or show events intended for everybody or just the Yelp community (Screenshot 11-19).

Idea #240: Get to Know the Anatomy of a Yelp Event Detail Page

On a Yelp event detail page you will find:

▲ Name of the event.

▲ Venue location.

▲ Ratings and reviews for the venue.

▲ Date of the event and an option to *"Add to Calendar."*

▲ Cost of the event.

▲ Map showing event location (links to Google Maps).

▲ RSVP buttons (*"I'm In!"* or *"Sounds Cool"*).

▲ Event description (*"What/Why"*).

▲ Button to share the event (*"Share event"*).

▲ Event discussion board (*"Discuss This Event"*).

▲ Listing of other Yelp members who said *"I'm In!"* or *"Sounds Cool."*

▲ Name of Yelp user who submitted the event.

▲ *"Nearby businesses"* and reviews.

▲ *"Other events this week."*

Idea #241: RSVP and Cancel an RSVP to a Yelp Event

To RSVP for a Yelp Event:

1. Sign up and register for a Yelp account if you don't already have one.

2. Go to any Yelp event detail page.

3. Click the button that says *"I'm In!"* to tell the organizer you are going.

   ✦ The event page will change to say *"You Replied I'm In!"*

   ✦ The event will now appear under your *"Upcoming Events"* on the Yelp *"Events"* page (right side of the page under *"Add an Event"*).

   ✦ An event update will be posted on the *"Events"* page (left-hand side under *"Event Spotlight"*) letting everyone know you have RSVP'd.

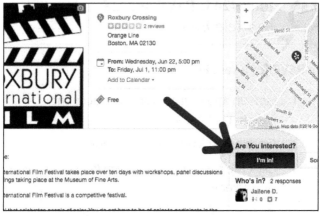

Screenshot 11-20

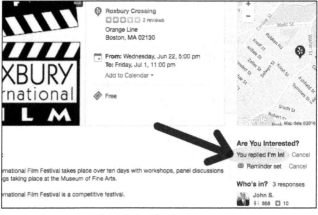

Screenshot 11-21

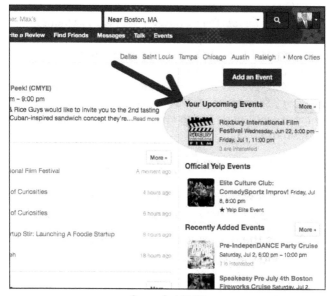

Screenshot 11-22

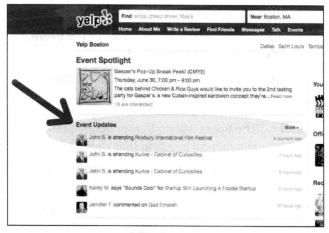

Screenshot 11-23

To RSVP for a Yelp event, find the event you want to attend. Click the "I'm In!" button on the event detail page (right side of the screen under the map of the event; Screenshot 11-20). The event page will now say "You Replied I'm In!" (Screenshot 11-21). The event will now appear under your "Upcoming Events" on the Yelp "Events" page (right side of the page under "Add an Event"; Screenshot 11-22). An event update will be posted on the "Events" page letting everyone know you have RSVP'd (Screenshot 11-23).

To Cancel Your RSVP to a Yelp Event:

1. Follow the steps in Ideas #236-#237 and go to a Yelp *"Events"* page.

2. On the right side of the Yelp *"Events"* page, find the section heading that says *"Your Upcoming Events."*

3. Click the name of the event you want to cancel your RSVP for and go to the Yelp event detail page for that event.

4. On the Yelp event detail page for the event, click *"Cancel"* (next to *"I'm In!"*).

   ✦ The *"I'm In!"* and *"Sounds Cool"* boxes will reappear on the page.

   ✦ The event will no longer be listed under the section heading that says *"Your Upcoming Events"* on the Yelp *"Events"* page.

   ✦ An event update will not be posted on the *"Events"* page when canceling an RSVP.

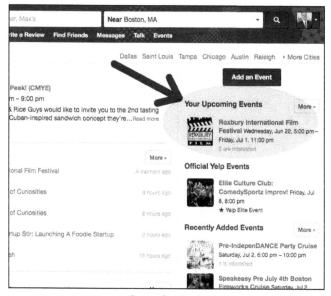

Screenshot 11-24

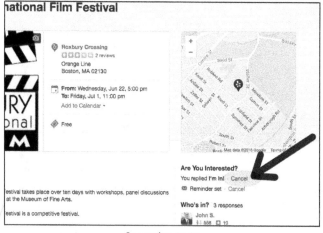

Screenshot 11-25

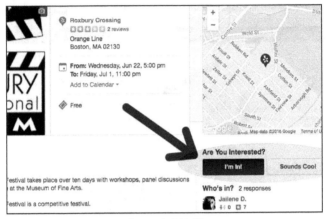

Screenshot 11-26

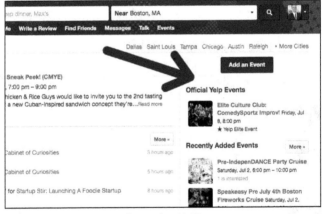

Screenshot 11-27

To cancel your RSVP for a Yelp event, follow the steps in Ideas #236-#237 and go to a Yelp "Events" page. On the right side of the Yelp "Events" page, find the section heading that says "Your Upcoming Events" (Screenshot 11-24). Click the name of the event you want to cancel your RSVP for and go to the Yelp event detail page for that event. On the Yelp event detail page for the event, click "Cancel" (next to "I'm In!"; Screenshot 11-25). The "I'm In!" and "Sounds Cool" boxes will reappear on the page (Screenshot 11-26). The event will no longer be listed under the section heading that says "Your Upcoming Events" on the Yelp "Events" page (Screenshot 11-27).

 ## Idea #242: Know How to Use <u>Yelp.com</u> to Create New Events

1. Go to the Yelp "*Events*" page for the city you want to post your event.

2. Click the *"Add an Event"* button (upper right corner of the screen).

3. Enter all the event details:

    ✦ Event name

    ✦ When

    ✦ Where

      • Name of public venue or private address

    ✦ Business name and the city the business is near

    ✦ What & Why

      • The reason to attend the event

    ✦ Who the event is for:

      • Everybody

      • Yelp Community

✦   Official Website URL

✦   Tickets URL

✦   Price of tickets

✦   Category of event

4. Click the *"Create Event"* button (bottom of
    the page) to submit your event for review
    and for posting.

Screenshot 11-28

Screenshot 11-29

To "Add an Event" on Yelp, go to the "Events" page for the city you want to add your event. Click the "Add an Event" button (upper right corner of the screen; Screenshot 11-28). Complete the "Submit an event" form (Screenshot 11-29).

 ## Idea #243: Know Who Your Yelp Community Manager (CM) Is

▲ Go to the Yelp Elite page at http://www.yelp.com/elite

▲ Find the section heading on the page that says *"Meet your Community Manager"* (left side of the page under header photo).

▲ Click the Community Manager's (CM) name and go to their profile page.

▲ On the CM's profile page you can learn more details about their interests, read reviews they have written, and also send them a message.

Screenshot 11-30

Screenshot 11-31

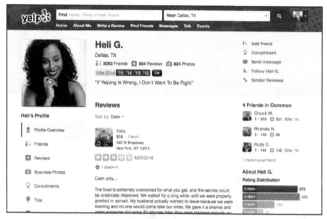

Screenshot 11-32

Locate your Yelp Community Manager (CM) by going to http://www.yelp.com/elite (Screenshot 11-30). Scroll down the page to find the section that says "Meet your Community Manager." In this section, locate the name of your CM (Screenshot 11-31) and click on their name to view their Yelp profile page (Screenshot 11-32).

 ## Idea #244: Identify the Yelp Community Manager (CM) for Another City

▲   Go to the Yelp Elite page at http://www.yelp.com/elite

▲   Click *"Not in [city name]"* (upper right corner of the screen).

▲   Select a city from the pop-up box.

▲   Follow the steps in Idea #243 to view the

community manager's profile page, where you can find out more about them and send them a message.

Screenshot 11-33

Screenshot 11-34

To find the Yelp Community Manager for another city, click "Not In [city name]" on http://www.yelp.com/ (Screenshot 11-33). Choose another city from the pop-up box that appears (Screenshot 11-34). Follow the steps in Idea #243 to find the new city's Yelp Community Manager.

Idea #245: Keep up with "The Local Yelp" for Cities You Are Interested In

▲ Go to the website yelp.com/weekly

▲ Select the city you want to receive "*The Local Yelp*" emails for.

    ✦ A listing of cities will appear (upper right of the screen under the top red nav menu).

    ✦ Select a city on the list or click "*More Cities*" (at the end of the list).

    ✦ Click "*More Locations*" (bottom of the "Other Local Yelp Locations" list) for a list of even more locations to choose from.

▲ Click on the "*Get It*" button (right side of the screen) on "*The Local Yelp*" page for your city of choice.

▲ Log back in to Yelp with your username and password to subscribe.

OR:

▲ Go to *"Account Settings"* by clicking on your profile picture (top right-hand corner of the screen).

▲ Select *"Email/Notifications"* (left side of the page under the Account Settings menu).

▲ Log back in to Yelp with your username and password.

▲ Look under *"Notification Settings"* for a section that says "From Yelp" (mid center of the page).

▲ Click/check the box next to *"The Local Yelp."*

▲ If needed, edit the desired city name.

Screenshot 11-35

Screenshot 11-35: To get "The Local Yelp" for a city you are interested in, go to yelp.com/weekly. After locating the city, click on the "Get It" button (right side of the screen). Log back in to Yelp with your username and password to subscribe.

Idea #246: Share Your Advice About Yelp Events

▲ Have you been to a Yelp event before?

▲ Do you have advice or want advice about going to Yelp events?

▲ Join our discussion on Yelp at *bit.ly/YelpEventsAdvice*

Screenshot 11-36

Share and get advice about Yelp events at bit.ly/YelpEventsAdvice

Idea #247: Use the Yelp Support Center to Get More Help with Yelp Events

1. Go to the website *yelp-support.com*

   OR:

2. Scroll down to the bottom of any Yelp page and click *"Support."*

   In the Yelp Support Center:

   ✦ Type the word *"Events"* into the search box and then click the button that says *"Search Support."*

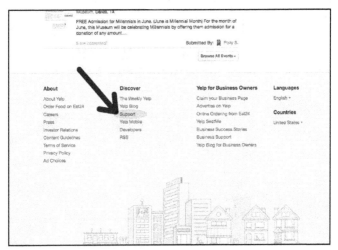

Screenshot 11-37

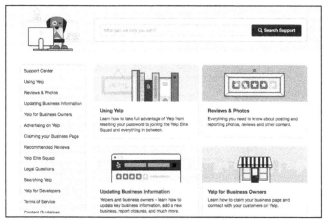

Screenshot 11-38

To get to the Yelp Support Center, go to the website yelp-support.com or scroll down to the bottom of any Yelp page and click "Support" (Screenshot 11-37). In the Yelp Support Center, type the word: "Events" into the search box, and then click the button that says "Search Support" to get more help with Yelp events (Screenshot 11-38).

PART 12

People, Events, and Fun with the Yelp App

 Idea #248: Understand How the Yelp App Works

▲ When it comes to events, the Yelp app is missing some key functionality that is available to users on the web-based version.

✦ The app works well in locating events in a user's current location. However, it does not allow users to access events taking place in other cities.

• The only way to view events in other cities is on the web-based version or by using the mobile app when you are in that city.

✦ Users cannot make changes to their home location using the Yelp app.

   • Changes to the default home location can only be made using the web-based version.

✦ Also, there's no way to *"Add an Event"* on the Yelp app.

   • The only way to create an event on Yelp is by using the web-based version.

 Idea #249: Understand How to Access the Yelp "Events" Page on the Yelp App

▲ Click the *"More"* button ☰ (bottom menu bar).

▲ Select *"Events"* from the *"More"* menu page.

▲ The Yelp *"Events"* page will appear where you will find:

   ✦ **My Upcoming events** (Events you have RSVP'd for).

   ✦ **Official Yelp events** (Events that don't have a waiting list or Elite events).

   ✦ **Popular events** (Unofficial Yelp Events).

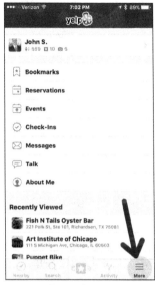

Screenshot 12-1   *Screenshot 12-2*

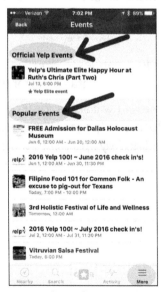

Screenshot 12-3

To Access the Yelp "Events" Page on the Yelp app, click the "More" button (bottom menu bar; Screenshot 12-1). Select "Events" from the "More" menu page (Screenshot 12-2). The Yelp "Events" page will appear where you will find: "My Upcoming Events," "Official Yelp Events," and "Popular Events" (Screenshot 12-3).

 ## Idea #250: Understand How to RSVP to an Event on the Yelp App

▲ Follow the steps in Idea #249 and go to the Yelp *"Events"* page.

▲ Click on any event under *"Official Yelp Events"* or *"Popular Events"* to go to the Yelp event detail page for the event.

▲ Click *"I'm In!"* or *"Sounds Cool"* on the event detail page to RSVP.

▲ After RSVP'ing for an event:

✦ *"I'm In!"* changes to *"You Replied: I'm In"* on the event detail page for the event.

✦ The event will also appear on the Yelp *"Events"* page under the section heading *"My Upcoming Events."*

Screenshot 12-4

Screenshot 12-5

Screenshot 12-6

Screenshot 12-7

Screenshot 12-8

To RSVP for an event using the Yelp app, click on any event under "Official Yelp Events" or "Popular Events" (Screenshot 12-4). The Yelp event detail page for that event will appear (Screenshot 12-5). Click "I'm In!" or "Sounds Cool" on the event detail page to RSVP (Screenshot 12-6). After RSVP'ing for the event, "I'm In!" changes to "You Replied: I'm In" (Screenshot 12-7). The event will also appear on the Yelp "Events" page under the section heading "My Upcoming Events" (Screenshot 12-8).

Idea #251: Know How to Use the Yelp App to Change Your RSVP for an Event

1. Follow the steps in Idea #249 and go to the Yelp "Events" page.

2. Find the section heading "My Upcoming Events."

3. Click the name of the event under "My Upcoming Events" that you want to change your RSVP to.

   ✦ The event detail page will appear for the event.

4. Click the down arrow ❤ (located to the right of "I'm In!" or "Sounds Cool") to change your RSVP.

5. Select "Cancel I'm In" to completely cancel your RSVP to the event.

   ✦ After making this selection, the event page will revert back to how it appeared before RSVP'ing to the event.

   ✦ The event will no longer appear on the "Events" page under "My Upcoming Events."

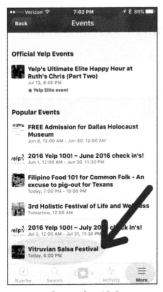

Screenshot 12-9

Screenshot 12-10

Screenshot 12-11

Screenshot 12-12

Screenshot 12-13

To change your RSVP for an event, click the name of the event under "My Upcoming Events" that you want to change your RSVP to (Screenshot 12-9). The event detail page for the event will appear. Select the down arrow (located to the right of "I'm In!" or "Sounds Cool"; Screenshot 12-10) to change your RSVP (Screenshot 12-11). To completely cancel the RSVP, choose "Cancel I'm In." After making this selection. the event page will revert back to how it appeared before RSVP'ing to the event (Screenshot 12-12). The event will no longer appear on the "Events" page under "My Upcoming Events" (Screenshot 12-13).

Idea #252: Be Familiar with How to Use the Yelp App to Send a Reminder or Notification About an Event

▲ Follow the steps in Idea #250 to RSVP for an event.

▲ After RSVP'ing for the event, make sure the "*Send Reminder*" switch is turned on.

▲ Enable notifications for the Yelp app in your phone's settings.

✦ iPhone users:

● Go to the Settings app.

● Click "*Notifications.*"

● Select "*Yelp.*"

● Turn on the notifications.

Screenshot 12-14

When using the Yelp app, make sure the "Send Reminder" switch is turned on (inside the event detail page) to receive notifications and reminders about the event.

 ## Idea #253: Understand How to Add a Yelp Event to Your Calendar

There are two ways to add an event from the Yelp app to your calendar (before or after RSVP'ing):

<u>First way</u>:

1. Go to any Yelp event detail page for an event you want to add.

2. Click the menu button represented by three dots ⟨···⟩ (right corner of the screen).

    ✦ A pop-up menu will appear (bottom of the screen).

3. Select *"Add to Calendar."*

    ✦ Choose the calendar you want to add the event to.

4. Select *"Done"* (upper right corner of the calendar page).

    ✦ Follow the prompts on the phone.

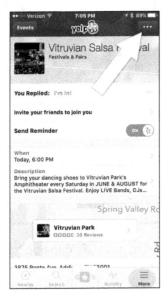

Screenshot 12-15   *Screenshot 12-16*

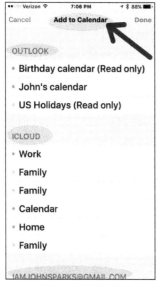

Screenshot 12-17   Screenshot 12-18

One way to add an event to your calendar is to go to an event detail page for the event and click the menu button represented by three dots (upper right corner; Screenshot 12-15). A pop-up menu will appear at the bottom of the screen. Select "Add to Calendar" (Screenshot 12-16). Choose the calendar you want to add the event to (Screenshot 12-17). Select "Done" (upper right corner of the calendar page; Screenshot 12-18) and then follow the prompts on the phone.

Second way:

1. Click the *right arrow* ❯ (located to the right of an event's date and time) on an event detail page.

2. Click *"Add to Calendar."*

    ✦ Select which calendar you want to add the event to.

3. Select *"Done"* (upper right corner of the calendar page).

    ✦ Follow the prompts on the phone.

Screenshot 12-19

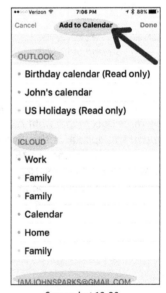

Screenshot 12-20

Screenshot 12-21

A second way to add an event to the calendar is to click the right arrow on an event detail page (located to the right of an event's date and time; Screenshot 12-19). Next, select the calendar you want to add the event to (Screenshot 12-20). Select "Done," and then follow the prompts on the phone (Screenshot 12-21).

Idea #254: Know How Use the Yelp App to Get an Event Description, a Link to the Event's Website, and a Link to Purchase Tickets to an Event

To get an event description, a link to the event's website, and a link to purchase tickets to an event:

- ▲ Click the *right arrow* ❯ adjacent to the event *"Description"* on a Yelp event detail page.

- ▲ A new page called *"Event Details"* will appear. On this page you will find:

  - ✦ An event description.

  - ✦ More dates and times of the event.

  - ✦ A link to get to the event's official website.

  - ✦ A link to purchase tickets, if tickets are for sale (bottom of the page).

Screenshot 12-22   Screenshot 12-23

To get an event description, a link to the event's website, and a link to get tickets to an event click the right arrow adjacent to the event "Description" (Screenshot 12-22). A page called "Event Details" will appear with the information you are looking for (Screenshot 12-23).

Idea #255: Learn How to View a Map of an Event's Location

▲ Go to any Yelp event detail page (before or after you RSVP for an event).

▲ Click either the map (located on the bottom of the page) or click the *right arrow* ❯ (located next to the address of

the event location) on any event detail
page.

✦   After clicking the map, click *"Open
    Maps App"* (upper right corner) to get
    driving directions or click the *compass
    icon* (bottom right corner) to open the
    location in compass view.

Screenshot 12-24   Screenshot 12-25

*To view a map of an event's location, click on the map or click
the right arrow next to the address of the event location on any
event detail page (Screenshot 12-24). Next, click "Open Maps
App" (upper right corner) for driving directions or click the
compass icon (bottom right corner) to view the map of the event
in compass view (Screenshot 12-25).*

Idea #256: Know How to Use the Yelp App to Get Directions to an Event

▲ Scroll down any Yelp event detail page and locate the word *"Directions."*

　✦ Underneath the word *"Directions,"* it will show you how many minutes it will take you to reach the event from your current location.

▲ Click on the word *"Directions"* to launch the phone's *"Maps"* app to get driving, walking, and transit directions.

Screenshot 12-26

Screenshot 12-27

To get directions to an event, scroll down on a Yelp event detail page and locate the word "Directions" (Screenshot 12-26). Underneath the word "Directions," it will show you how many minutes it will take you to reach the event from your current location. Click on the word "Directions." The "Maps" app will launch where you can get step-by-step driving, walking, and transit directions (Screenshot 12-27).

Idea #257: Know Where to Find Ratings, Reviews, and Contact Information for the Venue Where an Event Is Located

▲ Follow the steps in Idea #249 to get to the Yelp *"Events"* page.

▲ Click on any event under *"My Upcoming Events"*, *"Official Yelp Events"*, or *"Popular Events"* to go to the Yelp event detail page for that event.

▲ Click on the venue name that is located on the map on the event detail page.

▲ On the *"Venue"* page:

  ✦ See ratings, reviews, and contact information for the venue where an event is located.

  ✦ Write a review about the venue.

  ✦ Post a photo or video.

  ✦ Check in at the venue.

  ✦ Bookmark the page.

✦ Get directions, call, or message the venue.

Screenshot 12-28   Screenshot 12-29

To find ratings, reviews, and contact information for the venue where an event is located click on the venue name that is located on the map on the event detail page (Screenshot 12-28). The "Venue" page will appear (Screenshot 12-29). In addition to finding ratings, reviews, and contact information on this page, you can write a review about the venue, post a photo, and check in among other activities.

Idea #258: Post Comments on the Yelp App About an Event

▲ Scroll down any Yelp event detail page and find *"Discuss This Event."*

▲ Click on *"Discuss This Event"* to go to the *"Event Comments"* page where you can view and write comments about an event.

Screenshot 12-30

Screenshot 12-31

To view and write comments about an event, scroll down any Yelp event detail page and find "Discuss This Event" (Screenshot 12-30). Click "Discuss This Event" and the "Event Comments" page will appear (Screenshot 12-31).

Idea #259: Understand How to Use the Yelp App to View Others Who Have RSVP'd to an Event and See Their Profiles

▲ Scroll down any Yelp event detail page and find the section heading: *"Interested in This Event."*

   ✦ Under this section heading, you will find a partial list of users who have RSVP'd *"I'm In!"* or *"Sounds Cool."*

▲ Click the *right arrow* ❯ (located to the right of *"# are interested"*) to get to the *"Interested"* page.

▲ On the "Interested" page, click any user who has said *"I'm In!"* or *"Sounds Cool"* to see their Yelp profile.

Screenshot 12-32

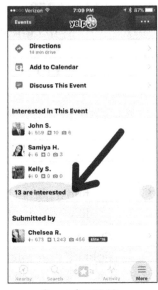

Screenshot 12-33

Screenshot 12-34

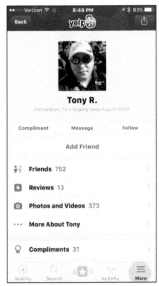

Screenshot 12-35

To view others who have RSVP'd for an event, scroll down any Yelp event detail page (Screenshot 12-32) and find the section heading "Interested in This Event." Click the right arrow (located to the right of "# are interested") to get to the "Interested" page (Screenshot 12-33). On the "Interested" page, view all users who have RSVP'd "I'm In!" and "Sounds Cool" (Screenshot 12-34). Click on the name of anyone who has RSVP'd. Their Yelp profile page will appear (Screenshot 12-35).

Idea #260: View the Profile of the User Who Submitted an Event

▲ Scroll down any Yelp event detail page and find the section heading *"Submitted by" (located underneath "Interested in This Event").*

▲ Click the *right arrow* ❯ (located to the right of the organizer's name) to view the organizer's Yelp profile.

| Screenshot 12-36 | Screenshot 12-37 |

To view the profile of the user who submitted an event, scroll down any Yelp event detail page and find the section heading "Submitted by" (Screenshot 12-36). Underneath, you will find the organizer's name. Click the right arrow (located to the right of the organizer's name). The organizer's Yelp profile page will appear (Screenshot 12-37).

Idea #261: Understand How to Use the Yelp App to Share an Event on Other Social Networks

▲   Share an event on the Yelp app by clicking the menu button represented by three dots [**···**] (upper right corner).

▲ A pop-up menu will appear at the bottom of the screen.

▲ Click *"Share Event"* on the pop-up menu.

▲ Share the event by:

✦ Email

✦ SMS (text message)

✦ AirDrop

✦ Other social media networks

Screenshot 12-38

Screenshot 12-39

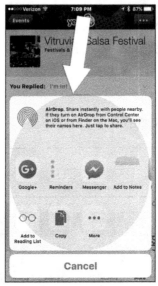

Screenshot 12-40

To share a Yelp event on other social networks, click the menu button represented by three dots (upper right corner; Screenshot 12-38). A pop-up menu will appear at the bottom of the screen. Click "Share Event" on the pop-up menu (Screenshot 12-39). Share the event via email, SMS (text message), Airdrop, or other social media networks (Screenshot 12-40).

Idea #262: Use the Yelp Support Center to Get More Help with Yelp Events

▲ Click the "*More*" button ☰ (bottom menu bar).

▲ The "*More*" menu page will appear.

▲ Scroll down the "*More*" menu page and find the section heading that says "*More.*"

▲ Underneath the "*More*" section heading, locate and click "*Support.*" ⊗

▲ The Yelp "*Support Center*" page will appear.

▲ Type the word "*Events*" in the search box on the "Support Center" page.

▲ Next, click the "*Search Support*" button to get more help and support with Yelp events.

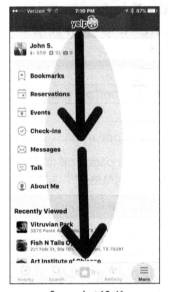

Screenshot 12-41

Screenshot 12-42

Screenshot 12-43

To get more help and support with Yelp events, click the "More" button (bottom menu bar, Screenshot 12-41). The "More" menu page will appear. Scroll down the "More" menu page and find the section heading that says "More." Underneath the "More" section heading, locate and click "Support" (Screenshot 12-42). The Yelp "Support Center" page will appear (Screenshot 12-43). Type the word "Events" in the search box and click the button which says "Search Support."

PART 13

Hang out at Events with Confidence with Google+

 Idea #263: Use Google+ to Find and Join Events on the Web

Google+ is the place to go if you're looking to genuinely engage with users at their events.

▲ Users say, since Google+ is owned by Google search and has a beautiful user interface that, it's the place to be.

▲ Those who use Google+ Tools (Hangouts in Real-life, Hangouts, and Hangouts On Air) say they can be quite captivating and appealing.

▲ Fans of Google+ say you can get away with only having Google+ for your internet life and that having one sign-on is all you need.

Google+ is one of the most spam-sensitive platforms and also one of the most hyper-sensitive about genuine engagement.

▲ **Access Google+ events by going to the Google+ website at:**

https://plus.google.com

Idea #264: Understand the Ups and Downs of Google+ Events

Ups:

▲ Events are a part of Google+, which is owned by Google. Google is a top competitor of Facebook. To continue to compete with Facebook, Google will continue to offer the same services or better to its users.

▲ Google understands the importance of live video streaming. With the recent popularity of Facebook Live, Google knows it must continue to make live video accessible to its users if the company is going to survive.

▲ Google realizes one of their core strengths has been their ability to make and provide an outlet where group interactions between larger communities is possible via live video streaming.

Downs:

▲ The future of Google+ which currently houses Google+ Events appears to be hanging in limbo.

▲ For Google to compete with Facebook, Google will have to continue to make more changes. Users will have to keep up with these changes to reap the benefits of these services.

✦ As this book is being printed, Google has announced Hangouts On Air (a type of Google+ Event) is moving from Google+ to YouTube Live. HOA Events can no longer be scheduled on Google+.

✦ Google also recently made changes to their Google+ mobile apps.

• With these changes, Google+ users can only access and use Google+ Events by switching back to "Classic Google+" on the web-based version or by using the Android app.

• Google+ events are no longer accessible on the iPhone.

Integration between Google+ events and Google Calendar can be both a plus and a minus:

▲ The integration is a plus for event organizers because Google+ Events sync with the Google Calendar. Furthermore, events are automatically added to the calendars of everyone they invite.

▲ Organizers like this as they can make sure their event is on the calendar of everyone they invite.

▲ The integration can be a real minus (and headache) for everyone else because events you're not expecting or interested in can get added to your calendar, without any notice, and have to be deleted.

 ## Idea #265: Understand What Google+ Events Are

▲ Just like the events on other websites and apps, Google+ Events can be just about anything one thinks up.

▲ Events can be parties, baby showers, receptions, conferences, office get-togethers, etc.

Idea #266: Know How to Find Google+ Events Online

Follow these steps to get to Google+ Events:

1. Go to the Google+ website:
   https://plus.google.com

2. Scroll down and click "*Back to Classic G+*" (bottom left-hand corner of the screen).

3. On the "*Classic Google+*" homepage, click the drop-down nav menu (upper left corner of the screen).

4. Select "*Events*" on the drop-down nav menu and the Google+ Events page will appear.

Screenshot 13-1

To get to Google+ Events, click the drop-down nav menu on the "Classic Google+" homepage (upper left corner of the screen). Select "Events" on the drop-down nav menu and the Google+ Events page will appear.

Idea #267: Get to Know the Types of Google+ Events

Up until the printing of this book, the most common types of events on Google+ have been Hangouts In Real-life (HIRL), Hangouts, and Hangouts On Air (HOA).

Since Hangouts On Air (HOA) is now moving to You-Tube Live, the two types of event listings you could find posted on your Google+ home feed are Hangouts In Real-life (HIRL) and Hangouts.

Idea #268: Understand the Differences between the Types of Google+ Events

Hangouts In Real-life (HIRL):

▲ Events people will attend live and in-person.

Hangouts:

▲ Video calls, phone calls, or messages.

▲ Accommodate up to ten people at a time.

▲ The public is not invited to attend (unless they are asked to join and have a link to join).

▲ The only users who can see or hear what is taking place in a Hangouts room are those participating in the video chat.

▲ Once Hangouts are over, they are *not* converted into YouTube videos.

Hangouts On Air (HOA):

▲ Live-streaming events.

▲ HOAs are no longer scheduled on Google+ and are scheduled on YouTube Live.

▲ To set up Hangouts On Air with YouTube Live, go to: https://support.google.com/youtube/answer/7083786?p=live_hoa&rd=1

Idea #269: Understand How Event Listings Were Made Simpler On the Google+ Events Page

Event listings just got a whole lot simpler on the Google+ "Events" page. Where users would once have to figure out if an event was a Hangout in Real-life event or a Hangout On Air (live-streaming video event), the only events that are now listed on the events page itself are Hangouts in Real-life.

For now, both HIRLs and Hangouts continue to appear from time to time on the Google+ home feed.

Idea #270: Know How to Tell If an Event on the Google+ Event Is a Hangouts in Real-Life (HIRL) Event or a Hangout

Hangouts In Real-life (HIRL):

- ▲ Postings appear on the Google+ "Events" page.

- ▲ Postings have the name of an event venue on them (under the date of the event).

- ▲ Postings have the address of an event venue on them (displayed when hovering over the event venue's name).

- ▲ Postings do not have the *Google Hangout icon* 💬 on them.

Hangouts:

- ▲ Postings do not appear on a Google+ "Events" page. Instead, they appear on a user's Google+ feed.

- ▲ Postings do not have the time or date on them.

- ▲ Postings have the *Google Hangout icon* 💬 on them and a link for others to join the Hangout (underneath the status update).

Idea #271: Get to Know the Anatomy of the Google+ Events Page

After you select *"Events"* from the Google+ nav menu (upper left corner of the screen), you will be taken to the *"Your Events"* page.

On the *"Your Events"* page:

▲ *"Upcoming events"* that you have RSVP'd to appear first.

▲ *"Declined events"* that you are not going to appear second.

▲ *"Past events"* that have already happened appear last.

If there are not any *"Upcoming events"* or *"Declined Events,"* then the "Past Events" will appear first on the page.

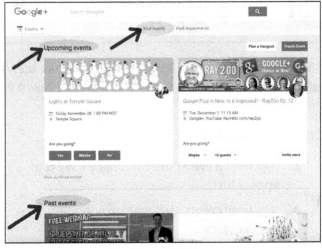

Screenshot 13-2

"Your Events" page shows "Upcoming events" (top of the page) and "Past events" (bottom of the page).

 ## Idea #272: Understand How to Remove Upcoming Events, Declined Events, and Past Events

1. Hover over the image for any event.

2. A pop-up ✖ will appear (top right corner of the image).

3. Click the pop-up ✖ and the event will be removed.

Idea #273: Learn How To *"Find More Events"* on Google+

1. Select *"Events"* from the Google+ drop-down nav menu (upper left corner of the screen).

2. Choose the *"Find more events"* tab (top center of the Google+ Events page).

3. Once on the *"Find more events"* tab, toggle between *"Best of"* and *"Most recent"* events by clicking the *down arrow* ❤ (located on the header at the top of the page).

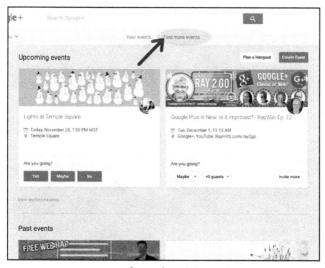

Screenshot 13-3

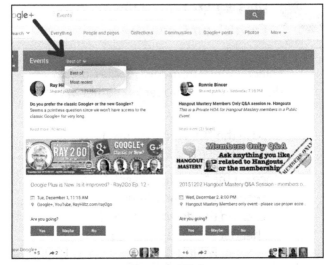

Screenshot 13-4

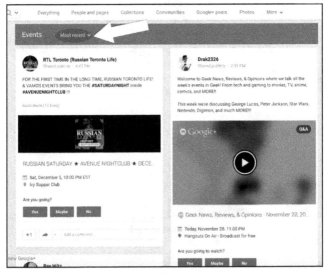

Screenshot 13-5

To find more events on Google+, choose the "Find more events" tab (top center of the Google+ Events page; Screenshot 13-3). Click the down arrow to toggle between "Best of events" and "Most recent" events (located on the header at the top of the page; Screenshot 13-4). Selecting "Most recent" displays the "Most recent" events page (Screenshot 13-5).

Idea #274: Understand Where to Go to Manage Event Listings on the *"Find More Events"* Page

▲ Hover the cursor over any event on the page.

▲ Look for the *down arrow* ⌄ to appear (top right corner of an event box).

▲ Click the *down arrow* ⌄ to manage your event listings on the *"Find More Events"* page.

Idea #275: Understand Your Options to Manage Event Listings on the "Find More Events" Page

▲ After clicking the *down arrow* ⌄ on any event on the "Find More Events" page, you will have the following options:

✦ View post activity *(only appears if there is activity on a post).*

- View a listing of anyone who has responded with a +1, commented on, or shared an event.

  - ✧ Add these people to your Google+ circles.

✦ Link to post

- Get a link to the post to share on social media or a website.

✦ Mute post

- Stop receiving notifications about an event.

✦ Report this post

- Report a post which appears to be inappropriate.

  - ✧ Google+ reviews the post and may remove the post or ban the user.

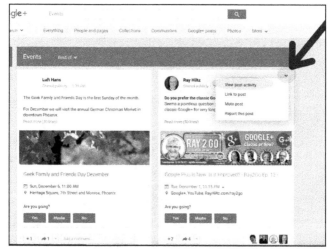

Screenshot 13-6

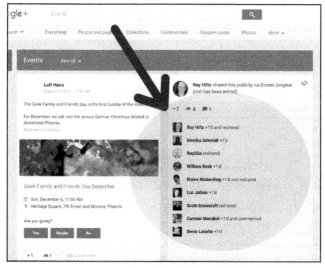

Screenshot 13-7

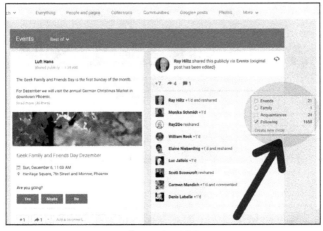

Screenshot 13-8

To manage your event listings on the "Find More Events" page, hover over any event listing and click on the down arrow. Select from the options to "View post activity," get a "Link to post," "Mute post," or "Report this post" (top right corner of the event listing; Screenshot 13-6). Select "View post activity." A list of users who have given the event a +1 or have reshared or commented on the event will appear (Screenshot 13-7). Hover over the user's names to add these users to your circles on Google+ (Screenshot 13-8).

Idea #276: Check Your Google Calendar to See If You Have Other Events Scheduled Before RSVP'ing to an Event

▲ Choose an event you've not already RSVP'd for in the *"Find more events"* or *"Upcoming events"* listings.

▲ Click the upside-down triangle (located on
the event listing to the right of the event
date and time).

▲ You will see all the events you have on
your calendar and the date the event is
scheduled, so you'll know if there are any
scheduling conflicts.

Screenshot 13-9

*To check your Google Calendar before RSVP'ing for an event,
select the upside-down triangle (located to the right of the event
date and time on the "Find more events" or "Upcoming events"
listings).*

Idea #277: RSVP to an Event From the "Find More Events" Listings Page

To RSVP for an event on the *"Find more events"* listings page, click the drop-down menu and choose:

- ▲ Yes
- ▲ Maybe
- ▲ No

By clicking *"Yes,"* a new box will appear that will allow you to add guests or *"Invite more"* to attend. The event will also show up on *"Your Events"* page, under the *"Upcoming events"* section heading.

Idea #278: Understand How To Get To A Google+ Event Detail Page From the Google+ Listings Page

To get to a Google+ event detail page, click on either:

1. An event theme image.
2. The title of any event.

Idea #279: Get to Know the Anatomy of a Google+ Event Detail Page

On the event detail page for a Google+ event is a(n):

▲ Event theme image/graphic/banner (top of the page, center).

▲ Event header, including:

✦ The title of the event.

✦ +1's the event has received.

✦ "Share event" box to click and share the event with other members and circles on Google+ or by email address.

▲ RSVP ("Are you going?").

▲ Event details ("Details"):

✦ Date and time of the event.

✦ Location (HIRL event).

✦ Event description

✦ Listings of panelists (HOA events).

▲ A listing of guests who are:

✦ Going

✦ Maybe

✦ Not Responded

▲ Event discussion board where you can say something about the event.

Idea #280: Know How to Create a Hangouts In Real-life (HIRL) Event on Google+ That Others Can Attend

1. Select *"Events"* from the Google+ drop-down nav menu (upper left corner of the screen) to go to the Google+ Events page.

2. Click the *"Create Event"* button (top right-hand corner of the screen on the Google+ Events page).

3. A pop-up box will appear to create your event.

4. Click *"Change Theme"* (located inside the picture at the top of the pop-up box) and select a theme for the event.

    ✦   Use a Google+ picture or upload your own.

5. Enter the event title, location, and details of the event in the pop-up box.

6. To enter a website URL, YouTube URL, and transit/parking information for your event, click the *"Event Options"* button (upper right-hand corner of the pop-up box; underneath the event picture). Next, select *"Advanced"* and *"Show More Options."* from the drop-down menu. New fields will appear in the pop-up box to enter your additional information.

7. Invite others to attend by entering names, Google+ circles, or email addresses inside the field that says "To:" (bottom of the pop-up box).

8. Click the *people icon* 👥 (next to the field that says "To:") and "Browse people" to invite.

9. Click on "*Invite*" to post and send out invites to the event (bottom left corner of the pop-up box).

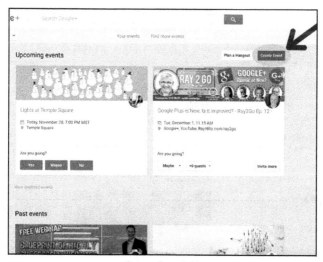

Screenshot 13-10

Screenshot 13-11

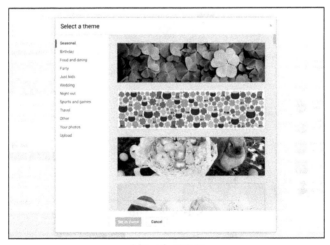

Screenshot 13-12

Screenshot 13-13

Screenshot 13-14

Screenshot 13-15

To create a Hangouts In Real-life (HIRL) event on Google+, select "Events" from the Google+ drop-down nav menu (upper left corner of the screen) to go to the Google+ Events page. Click the "Create Event" button (top right-hand corner of the screen on the Google+ Events page; Screenshot 13-10). A pop-up box will appear to create your event. Click "Change Theme" (located inside the picture at the top of the pop-up box; Screenshot 13-11). Select a theme for the event (Screenshot 13-12). Use a Google+ picture or upload your own. Enter the event title, location, and details of the event in the pop-up box. To enter a website URL, YouTube URL, and transit/ parking information for your event, click the "Event Options" button on the pop-up box, followed by "Advanced" and "Show More Options." from the drop-down menu (Screenshot 13-13). Click the people icon (lower-right hand corner of the pop-up box; Screenshot 13-14) and the "Browse people" box will appear where you can "Browse people" to invite (Screenshot 13-15). After selecting the people to invite, click "Invite" on the original pop-up box to post and send out invites to the event.

Idea #281: Know How to Allow Guests to Invite Other People to an Event and Add Their Own Pictures to an Event Page

When creating an event, you can choose to allow guests to invite other people to the event and/or add their own pictures to the event page.

1. Follow steps #1-3 in Idea #280 to create a Hangouts In Real-life (HIRL) event.

2. Click the "Event Options" button (upper right-hand corner of the "Create Event" pop-up box; underneath the event picture).

3. Select "Basic" from the drop-down menu.

4. Click/check the box next to "Guests can invite other people" and "Guests can add photos."

5. Enter the rest of your event details.

6. Click on "Invite" to post and send out invites to the event (bottom left corner of the pop-up box).

▲ **To learn more about adding photos and videos to Google+ events, read:** https://support.google.com/plus/answer/2613195?hl=en

Screenshot 13-16

To allow guests to invite other people to the event and/or add their own pictures to the event page, select "Event options" (upper right-hand corner of the "Create Event" pop-up box; underneath the event picture). Select "Basic." from the drop-down menu. Click/check the box next to "Guests can invite other people" and "Guests can add photos."

Idea #282: Know How to Have a Google Hangout

▲ Select *"Hangouts"* from the Google+ drop-down nav menu (upper left corner of the screen).

▲ Click the green button on the next page which says *"Visit hangouts.google.com"*

OR:

▲ Click the *Google Hangout icon* 💬 on any Google+ page (top right of the screen; just underneath your profile image).

▲ Click the green button on the next page which says *"Visit hangouts.google.com"*

OR:

▲ Go to hangouts.google.com

Following these steps will take you to the Hangouts page where you can choose to make a video call, phone call, or message a user or group of users.

Screenshot 13-17

Screenshot 13-18

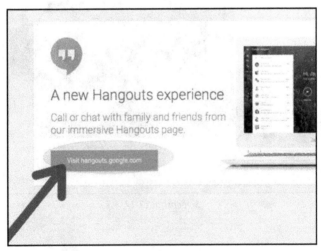

Screenshot 13-19

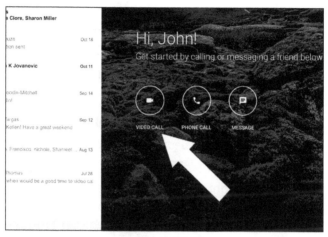

Screenshot 13-20

To have a Hangout the public is NOT invited to (and will NOT be recorded on YouTube), select "Hangouts" on the Google+ drop-down menu (Screenshot 13-17), or click the Google Hangout icon (top right of the screen, just underneath your profile picture; Screenshot 13-18). Click the green button on the next page which says "Visit hangouts.google.com" (Screenshot 13-19). Next, choose to make either a video call, phone call, or send a message from the Hangouts page (Screenshot 13-20). A pop-up box will appear. Invite people to join you by entering a contact's name or email address. You can also copy the link to the Hangout and share it with others so they can join.

Idea #283: Understand How to Invite People to Attend a Google Hangout

1. Go to http://hangouts.google.com

2. Select "*Video Call*" on the main Hangouts page.

3. Switch to the original version of Hangouts.

    ✦ Click the menu button represented by three dots ⋮ (upper right corner).

    ✦ Select *"Original version."* →

    ✦ A video box, permanent link, and *"Invite people"* button will appear.

4. Click the *"Invite people"* button and another pop-up box will appear.

5. On the right side of the pop-up box, click the red *"G+"* logo. A Google+ post will appear.

6. Copy and bookmark the permanent link on the new pop-up box, so you can use it to invite others and can always return to this Hangout.

7. Write a comment about the Hangout in the *"Add a comment"* section.

8. Choose who you want to be able to view your Hangout posting:

    ✦ By default, a Hangout post is set to be shared with the *"Public."*

    ✦ If you don't want this to be a post that everyone can see, remove *"Public."*

    ✦ Add circles, communities, email addresses, or names of people you want to view the post.

9. Click *"Share."*

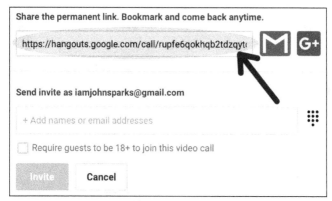

Screenshot 13-21

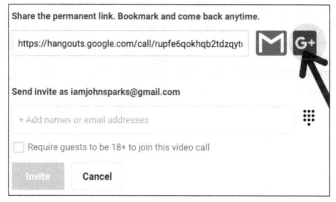

Screenshot 13-22

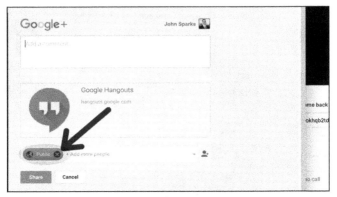

Screenshot 13-23

Invite the public (or others you choose) to a Hangout by going to hangouts.google.com. Switch to the original version of Hangouts by clicking the menu button represented by three dots (upper right corner). A video box, permanent link, and "Invite people" button will appear. Click the "Invite people" button. Copy and paste the Hangouts permanent link on the next pop-up box to invite others you choose to join the Hangout (Screenshot 13-21). Next, click the G+ logo (located to the right of the Hangouts permanent link) to create a post to share on your Google+ feed (Screenshot 13-22). Add "Public" to share your post with everyone on Google+, or select other circles of your choice (Screenshot 13-23).

 ## Idea #284: Understand How to Schedule a Google Hangout

1. Select *"Events"* from the Google+ drop-down nav menu (upper left corner of the screen).

2. From the events listing page, select the *"Plan A Hangout"* button *or "Create Event"* button (top right of the screen).

+ If you select the *"Create Event"* button, when the next pop-up box appears to enter the event information, make sure to click the *"Event Options"* button, followed by *"Advanced"* and *"Hangouts"* from the drop-down menu.

3. Complete steps #4-9 in Idea #280 to finish posting and sending out invites for your event.

Screenshot 13-24

To schedule a Hangout using the "Create Event" button, make sure to click the "Event Options" button (upper right-hand corner of the "Create Event" pop-up box; underneath the event picture) Next, select "Advanced" and "Show More Options." from the drop-down menu."

Idea #285: Know When to Post a Google+ Event as a *"Public"* Post

▲ When creating postings for events in Google + Events that you want everyone to see, make sure to add *"Public"* to the *"To"* field before posting it for the very first time on Google+.

✦ After posting an event, you cannot edit the event and make the event a *"Public"* event. Instead, the event will have to be re-created and re-posted with *"Public"* in the *"To:"* field.

✦ Only users who are members of certain circles will be able to view an event that is not marked *"Public."*

✦ Events not marked *"Public"* are difficult for others to share.

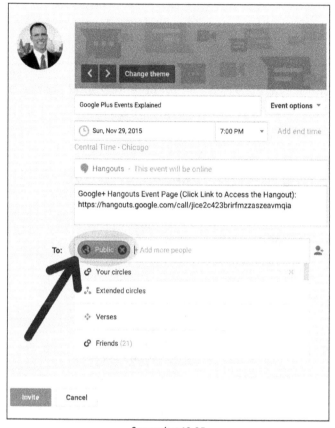

Screenshot 13-25

If you want everyone to be able to see your event postings on Google+, make sure to add "Public" in the "To:" field before posting it for the very first time After posting an event, you cannot edit the event and make the event a "Public" event. Instead, the event will have to be re-created and re-posted with "Public" in the "To:" field.

Idea #286: Understand How to Change an Event to Make It "Public" on Google+

The only way to make an event "Public" after posting it is by deleting the event and starting over.

Idea #287: Know How to Post an Event in a Google+ Community

▲   When creating postings for Google+ Events, enter the name of the community in the "To:" field before posting the event for the first time to Google+.

▲   When adding an event to "Community Circles," the event will appear on a Community's Special Events page.

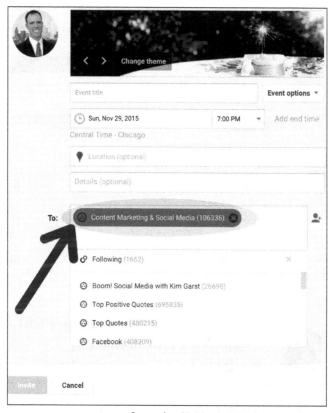

Screenshot 13-26

Enter the name of a community in the "To:" field before posting the event for the first time to Google+.

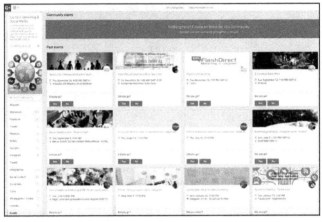

Screenshot 13-27

Event listings that are shared with communities will appear on the community's special events page.

Idea #288: Warning: You Can't Edit a Google+ Event to Make It Available on a Community Page

▲   After posting an event, you cannot edit the event and add additional communities.

▲   Just like with "*Public*" events, the only way to add a community after posting an event is to delete the event and start over. Therefore, be sure to enter the names of *all* the desired communities in the "To:" field before finalizing your post.

Idea #289: Understand What Happens When You Delete a Google+ Event

▲ The event is deleted and does not appear on anyone's event listings page.

▲ The event does not appear on any public or private streams on Google+.

▲ The event is deleted from all of the calendars it was added to.

▲ Comments about the event and photos taken at the event are no longer visible or accessible.

 ## Idea #290: Know How to Delete a Google+ Event

1. Select *"Events"* from the main Google+ drop down nav menu (upper left corner of the screen under the Google+ logo).

   ✦ You will be taken to the *"Your Events"* page.

2. Locate the event you created and want to delete under *"Upcoming events."* Click the event title.

   ✦ You will be taken to the event detail page for that event.

3. Click the *down arrow* ∨ located to the left
    of the "*Details*" section on the event detail
    page.

4. Select *"Delete this event"* from the drop-
    down menu.

5. When prompted, confirm you want to
    delete the event.

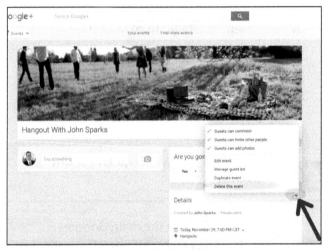

Screenshot 13-28

Screenshot 13-29

To delete an event, locate the event detail page for an event you created and want to delete. Click the down arrow located to the left of the "Details" section on the event detail page. Select "Delete this event" from the drop-down menu (Screenshot 13-28). When prompted, confirm you want to delete the event (Screenshot 13-29).

 ## Idea #291: Getting More out of Google+ Events

To get more out of Google+ events, check out the following resources:

▲   Google+ Official Help Page For Events: https://support.google.com/plus/ answer/2673334?hl=enAndref topic=2612996

Other helpful resources, including articles and videos, include:

- ▲ How To Create a Google+ Event [Quick Tip]: http://blog.hubspot.com/marketing/how-to-create-a-google-plus-event

- ▲ 5 Ways To Use Google+ Events For Your Business: http://www.socialmediaexaminer.com/google-plus-events/

PART 14

Create a Better World with Couchsurfing Events

 Idea #292:
Know What Couchsurfing Is!

▲ The Couchsurfing website has been around since 2003, but Couchsurfing itself has been around much longer than the website.

▲ "Surfing" is a term used for someone who is traveling from one city to another looking for whatever space is available to sleep on while they're in town.

▲ Couchsurfing users create interest profiles for networking with hopes of making friends and landing free accommodations when they're on the road.

▲ Couchsurfing probably isn't the site most people think of when they're looking for events to attend. Nevertheless, it's a great place to meet locals, as well as visitors from other cities.

▲ Events on Couchsurfing are accessible through the Couchsurfing website and the Couchsurfing app.

Idea #293: Understand Why You Should Consider Trying out Couchsurfing

▲ Couchsurfing events allow surfers to get to know and connect with future hosts before staying with them.

▲ Events can be invaluable networking and learning opportunities for all who attend.

✦ Users from different backgrounds and cultures come together offline to experience life together and explore similar interests.

▲ According to the Couchsurfing website, Couchsurfing's "free service connects travelers across the globe who share experiences ranging from hosting one another in their homes to becoming close friends and travel companions."

There are several ways you can try out Couchsurfing:

▲ **Couchsurfing is available on the web at:**
http://www.Couchsurfing.com

▲ **iPhone users can download the Couchsurfing app by going to:**
https://itunes.apple.com/us/
app/Couchsurfing-travel-app/
id525642917?mt=8

▲ **Android users can download the Couchsurfing app by going to:**
https://play.google.com/store/apps/
details?id=com.couchsurfing.mobile.
android&hl=en

Screenshot 14-1

Couchsurfing app in the Apple iTunes Store.

At the time this book was published, Couchsurfing reports they are a global network of over 10 million people in over 200,000 cities.

 Idea #294: Understand the Ups and Downs of Couchsurfing Events

Ups:

▲ Couchsurfing events cater to more diverse and eclectic crowds, including travelers and out-of-towners.

▲ Events are in a public setting where it's possible to get to know others in a safe way.

▲ Organizers are able to limit the number of attendees who can RSVP for an event and keep an event at a certain size.

▲ After an event is over, users can leave a reference for the event organizers.

▲ Events are a great way to cast out fear and feel safe about easing into the Couchsurfing experience.

Downs:

▲ Apart from major metro areas, which have large Couchsurfing communities (e.g., New York, Los Angeles, San Francisco), you may find there are not many Couchsurfing events in your city.

▲ At the time of publishing this book, there were 64 events listed in Chicago; 58 events in Los Angeles; 53 events in New York City; and 29 events in Seattle. At the same time, there were only six events in Houston and one event in Dallas.

 Idea #295: Know How to Use the Couchsurfing Web Version to Search for Events

1. To find events on Couchsurfing's web-based version, create an account and log in at http://www.Couchsurfing.com

2. Click on *"Events"* (top right of the screen, to the left of your profile picture on the Couchsurfing header/nav bar).

3. The Couchsurfing events listing page for your hometown will appear.

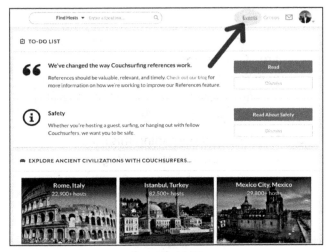

Screenshot 14-2

Screenshot 14-3

To find events on Couchsurfing's web-based version, create an account and log in at http://www.Couchsurfing.com. Click on "Events" (top right of the screen, to the left of your profile picture on the Couchsurfing header/nav bar; Screenshot 14-2). The Couchsurfing events listing page for your hometown will appear (Screenshot 14-3).

Idea #296: Know How to Use the Couchsurfing Web Version to View an Event Detail Page

▲ Click on *"Events"* (top right of the screen, to the left of the profile picture on the Couchsurfing header/nav bar).

▲ Click on the title of the event you wish to view.

▲ On the event detail page, you will find the following:

✦ Name of the event

✦ Who organized the event

✦ City the event will be held in

✦ *"Join Event"* button to RSVP

✦ Who else is going to the event

✦ Icons to share the event on social media

✦ Description of the event

✦ Place to post public comments about an event (comment thread)

Screenshot 14-4

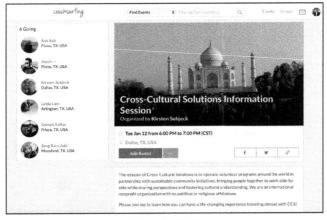

Screenshot 14-5

To get to an event detail page on Couchsurfing, click on "Events" (top right of the screen, to the left of your profile picture on the Couchsurfing header/nav bar). Next, click on the title of the event you wish to view (Screenshot 14-4). On the event detail page, you will find the following: name of the event, who organized the event, city the event will be held in, etc. (Screenshot 14-5).

Idea #297: Know How to RSVP to a Couchsurfing Event

▲ Click on the blue box that says *"Join event"* (located underneath the lower left corner of the event picture on a Couchsurfing event detail page).

▲ The *"Join Event"* box will now say *"I'm going."*

▲ Your name will appear on the event detail page (left-hand side) next to others who are also going to the event.

▲ The event will show up under the section heading *"My Upcoming Events"* (on the Couchsurfing homepage) and *"Events I'm Attending"* (lower left corner of the *"Events"* page).

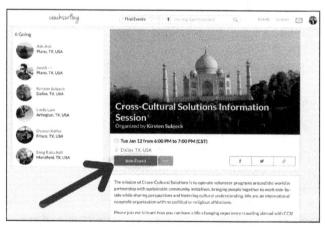

Screenshot 14-6

Screenshot 14-7

Screenshot 14-8

To RSVP for a Couchsurfing event, click "Join Event" on the event detail page (Screenshot 14-6). "Join Event" will change to "I'm going" (Screenshot 14-7). Events you are going to will appear under "Events I'm Attending" (lower left corner of the "Events" page; Screenshot 14-8).

Idea #298: Understand How to Add Couchsurfing Events to Your Calendar

1. RSVP to any event.

2. Click *"Add to Calendar"* (located underneath the lower right corner of the event picture on a Couchsurfing event detail page).

3. Select the calendar in the drop-down menu that you want to add your event to.

4. Choose to add only this event to the calendar or to *"Sync all Couchsurfing Activity."* Follow the prompts based on what you select.

Note: Couchsurfing only lets users add events to their calendar after they have RSVP'd for an event.

Screenshot 14-9

Screenshot 14-10

To add an RSVP'd event to the calendar, first RSVP to any event from a Couchsurfing event detail page. Next, click "Add to Calendar" and select the calendar in the drop-down menu that you want to add your event to (Screenshot 14-9). In the pop-up box that appears, choose to add only this event to the calendar or "Sync all Couchsurfing Activity" (Screenshot 14-10).

Idea #299: Know How to Discover More Details About Who Has Organized a Couchsurfing Event

▲ It's not necessary to RSVP for a Couchsurfing event to find out who's organizing the event, going to the event, view profiles of attendees, and send attendees a message.

✦ Go to any Couchsurfing event detail page.

✦ Locate *"Organized by"* (lower left corner of the event photo).

✦ Click the organizer's name to go to their Couchsurfing profile page.

✦ On the profile page, you will find the organizer's:

- Age
- Current location
- Occupation
- Education
- Interests
- Hometown
- References
- Languages spoken
- What they use Couchsurfing for
- Couchsurfing groups they belong to
- How long they've been on Couchsurfing
- Whether or not they're a verified Couchsurfing user
- If they're accepting Couchsurfing guests at their home

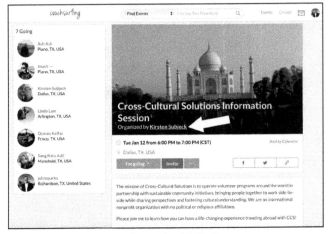

Screenshot 14-11

Screenshot 14-12

Click on the event organizer's name to go to an event organizer's profile (lower left corner of the event photo; Screenshot 14-11). On the event organizer's profile find details, including: age, current location, occupation, education, etc. (Screenshot 14-12).

Idea #300: Know How to Send a Message to the Organizer of a Couchsurfing Event

▲ Go to an organizer's profile page.

▲ Click the *"Message"* button 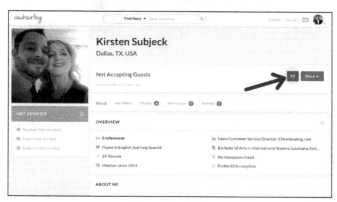 (right side of the page).

▲ A pop-up box will appear to send the organizer a message.

Screenshot 14-13

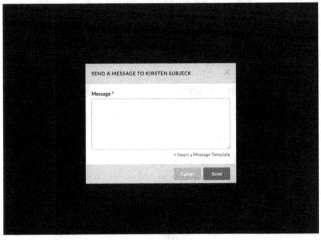

Screenshot 14-14

Click the "Message" button on an organizer's profile page (right side of the screen; Screenshot 14-13) to send the organizer of a Couchsurfing event a message. A pop-up box will appear allowing you to type and send your message (Screenshot 14-14).

Idea #301: Know How to Leave a Reference for the Organizer of a Couchsurfing Event

1. Click the button that says *"More"* on a user's profile page that you want to recommend.

2. Select *"Write Reference"* on the drop-down menu.

3. A pop-up box will appear to write a reference.

4. Choose from:
   - ✦ *"Yes, I'd recommend"*
   - ✦ *"No, I wouldn't recommend"*

5. Leave a comment in the section *"What was memorable about…"*

6. Click the *"Preview"* button (bottom right corner of the pop-up box).

7. Follow the prompts to submit your reference.

Screenshot 14-15

Screenshot 14-16

To leave a reference on Couchsurfing, locate a person's profile and click the button that says "More". Next, select "Write reference" on the drop-down menu (right side of the screen; Screenshot 14-15). A pop-up box will appear to write a reference. Choose "Yes, I'd Recommend" or "No, I wouldn't recommend" and leave a comment. Click the "Preview" button and follow the prompts to submit your reference (bottom right corner of the pop-up box; Screenshot 14-16).

Idea #302: Understand Why It's Always a Good Idea to Leave an Event Organizer a Reference

Leaving a Couchsurfing organizer a reference is a good idea because:

▲ Positive references may encourage other potential organizers to think about hosting events.

▲ When others become encouraged from seeing positive references and decide to host their own events, the number of events on Couchsurfing will increase.

▲ References can motivate other Couchsurfing members to want to engage with both the sender and receiver of these references.

Idea #303: Know How to Find out More Details About Others Who Say They're Going to a Couchsurfing Event

▲ Locate *"Going"* on any Couchsurfing event detail page (left side of the page).

▲ Click the name of one of the Couchsurfing members attending the event.

▲ The member's profile page will appear where you can learn more about event attendees before going to the event.

▲ Follow the Steps in Idea #300 and send a message to an attendee the same way you would send a message to an event organizer.

Screenshot 14-17

Screenshot 14-18

Go to any Couchsurfing event detail page, and look under "Going" to find out who else is going to an event (left side of an event detail page; Screenshot 14-17). Click any of the attendee's names who are attending an event to visit their profile page and send them a message before the event (Screenshot 14-18).

Idea #304: Understand How to Invite Friends on Couchsurfing to an Event

1. RSVP to any event.

2. Click the *"Invite"* button on any Couchsurfing event detail page (left of the page under the event photo and location).

3. A pop-up box will appear.

4. Check the boxes next to the friends you want to invite.

5. Click the *"Invite"* button on the pop-up box (bottom right corner) to send out invitations.

Screenshot 14-19

Screenshot 14-20

Click the "Invite" button to invite friends on Couchsurfing to an event (underneath the event photo on the left side; Screenshot 14-19). A pop-up box will appear (Screenshot 14-20). Check the boxes next to the friends you want to invite and click the "Invite" button on the pop-up box (bottom right corner) to send out invitations.

 ## Idea #305: Know How to Share a Couchsurfing Event on Social Media

▲ Click the Facebook or Twitter button (underneath the event photo on the right side).

✦ Once directed to Facebook or Twitter, decide how you want to share the link.

OR:

▲   Click the *"Link"* button (next to the Facebook and Twitter button).

✦   The link for the Couchsurfing event will be copied to your clipboard for you to use it however you decide.

Screenshot 14-21

To share a Couchsurfing event on social media, click the Facebook, Twitter, or "Link" button (underneath the event photo, on the right side) on a Couchsurfing event detail page.

Idea #306: Know How to View a List of All Couchsurfing Events You Are Attending

1. Click the Couchsurfing logo to go to the Couchsurfing Dashboard (upper left corner of any page).

2. On the Couchsurfing Dashboard, look under the section heading, *"My Upcoming Events."*

OR:

1. Click *"Events"* (top right of the screen, to the left of the profile picture on the Couchsurfing nav bar).

2. Look under *"Events I'm Attending"* (left side of the "Events" page).

Screenshot 14-22

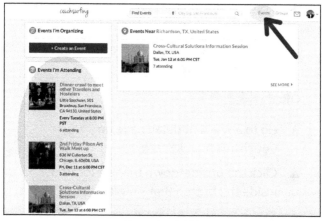

Screenshot 14-23

To view all the events you have RSVP'd for (1) Click the Couchsurfing logo (upper left corner of any page) to go to the Couchsurfing Dashboard. On the Couchsurfing Dashboard, look under the section heading, "My Upcoming Events" (Screenshot 14-22), or (2) click "Events" (top right of the screen, to the left of the profile picture on the Couchsurfing nav bar) to go to the "Events" page. On the "Events" page, look under "Events I'm Attending" (Screenshot 14-23).

 Idea #307: Know How to Cancel Your RSVP for a Couchsurfing Event

▲ Click the Couchsurfing logo to go to the Couchsurfing Dashboard (upper left corner of any page).

▲ On the Couchsurfing Dashboard, look under the section heading, *"My Upcoming Events."*

▲ Click the button that says *"Leave"* (located to the right of any event).

▲ Your RSVP has now been cancelled and the organizer will be informed.

OR:

▲ Go to any event detail page on Couchsurfing.

▲ Click the upside-down triangle located inside the button that says *"I'm going."*

▲ Select *"Leave."*

▲ Your RSVP has now been cancelled and the organizer will be informed.

After following these steps, the canceled event will no longer appear on the Couchsurfing Dashboard under *"My Upcoming Events"* or the event listings page under *"Events I'm Attending."*

Screenshot 14-24

Screenshot 14-25

To cancel an RSVP for a Couchsurfing event, either (1) find the event on the Couchsurfing Dashboard under the section heading "My Upcoming Events" and click the "Leave" button next to the event (Screenshot 14-24), or (2) click the upside-down triangle located inside the button that says "I'm going" on an event detail page and change it to "Leave" (Screenshot 14-25).

Idea #308: Know How to View and RSVP to Attend Couchsurfing Events in Other Cities

▲ Click the drop-down search box (top center of the Couchsurfing header/nav bar) and select "*Find Events.*"

▲ Type in the name of the city you're traveling to and then select the city name from the drop-down menu.

▲ A listing of Couchsurfing events will appear for that city.

✦ Sort events by date or by how many people are attending the event.

✦ Click the "*Join*" button (located to the right of the event listing) to RSVP for an event.

▲ Click the name of any event to go to the Couchsurfing event detail page for that event.

✦ On the event detail page, get a more in-depth description and see who's already going.

✦ Here, you can also RSVP for any event.

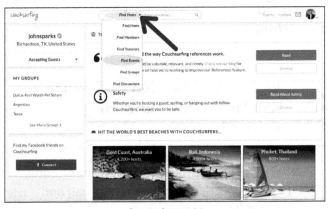

Screenshot 14-26

Screenshot 14-27

Screenshot 14-28

To view and RSVP for Couchsurfing events in other cities, click the drop-down search box (top center of the Couchsurfing header/ nav bar) and select "Find Events" (Screenshot 14-26). Type in the name of the city you're traveling to and then select the city name from the drop-down menu (Screenshot 14-27). A listing of Couchsurfing events will appear for that city (Screenshot 14-28). Sort events by date or by how many people are attending the event. Click the "Join" button (located to the right of the event listing) to RSVP for an event or click the name of any event to go to the Couchsurfing event detail page for that event.

Idea #309: Know How Change the Default Home Location for Events to Another Location

- ▲ Click the upside-down triangle (top right of any page, to the right of the profile picture on the Couchsurfing nav bar).

- ▲ Click *"Account & Settings"* on the drop-down menu.

- ▲ When the "Account & Settings" page appears, click *"Edit/Verify Your Location"* (mid-center of the page; under the *"Account Details"* section heading).

  - ✦ If *"Edit/Verify Your Location"* does not appear, then look for the *pencil icon*.

- ▲ A pop-up box will appear. Change your address in the pop-up box.

- ▲ Click *"Save"* to update the location.

Things To Know:

1. You can only change your address on the web-based version of <u>Couchsurfing.com</u>. You cannot change your address on the mobile app.

2. Once an address is changed on the Couchsurfing website, a postcard will be sent to your address to verify it.

3. If you're having trouble updating your address on the web-based version of Couchsurfing, go to Google Maps and get a link to the location.

4. If you're still having issues updating your address, submit a request through the Couchsurfing Help Center (See Idea #312).

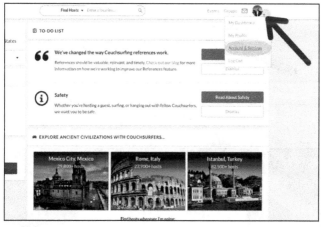

Screenshot 14-29

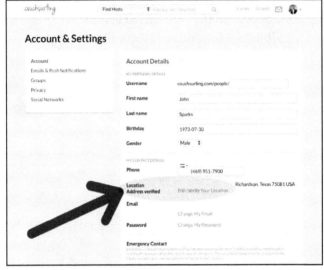

Screenshot 14-30

Screenshot 14-31

To change the default home location for events to another location, you must update your address in "Account & Settings." To update your address, click the upside-down triangle (top right of any page, to the right of your profile picture on the Couchsurfing nav bar; Screenshot 14-29). Click "Account & Settings" on the drop-down menu. On the "Account & Settings" page, click "Edit/Verify Your Location" (mid-center of the page; under the "Account Details" section heading; Screenshot 14-30). Update your address in the pop-up box that appears (Screenshot 14-31). Read Idea #309 for important information on verifying your address before completing this process.

Idea #310: Know How to Use Couchsurfing to Create and Delete Events

To create new events using Couchsurfing:

▲ Click "*Events*" (top right of the screen, to the left of the profile picture on the Couchsurfing nav bar).

▲ On the left-hand side of the "*Events*" page, click the "*Create an Event*" button.

▲ A pop-up box will appear. Type in the name, date, and location of the event. Limit the attendees if you want to keep the event small.

▲ Once you've entered the event details, click the *"Create Event"* button (lower right corner of the pop-up box).

▲ Add a photo for the event and click "*Save*" to post the event.

To delete events using Couchsurfing:

1. Click the Couchsurfing logo (upper left corner of any page) to go to the Couchsurfing homepage.

2. Locate the event you created under *"My Upcoming Events."*

3. Click the *"Edit"* button and a pop-up box will appear.

4. Scroll down and click *"Cancel Event."*

5. Confirm you want to cancel the event.

Screenshot 14-32

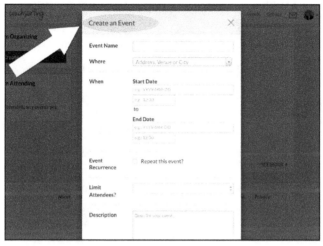

Screenshot 14-33

To create an event, click "Events" (top right of the screen, to the left of the profile picture on the Couchsurfing nav bar). On left-hand side of the "Events" page, click the "Create an Event" button (Screenshot 14-32). A pop-up box will appear. Type in the name, date, and location of the event. Limit attendees if you want to keep the event small (Screenshot 14-33). At the bottom of the pop-up box, click the "Create event" button. After, you will be prompted to add a photo for the event. Upload a photo and click "Save" to post the event.

 ## Idea #311: Understand How to Change/Adjust Emails and Push Notifications for Couchsurfing Events

▲ Click the upside-down triangle (top right of any page, to the right of the profile picture on the Couchsurfing nav bar).

▲ Click *"Account & Settings"* on the drop-down menu.

▲ On the *"Account & Settings"* page, click *"Emails & Push Notifications"* (left-hand side menu).

▲ Select the updates you want to receive and how you want to receive them (Email or Push) by making selections under "Email & Push Communications."

▲ Click the *"Save Changes"* button at the bottom of the page to save your selections.

Screenshot 14-34

Screenshot 14-35

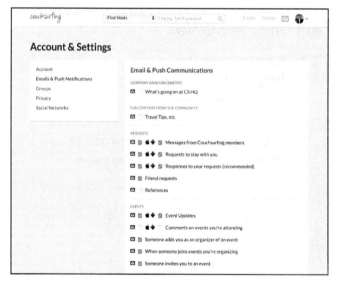

Screenshot 14-36

To change/adjust emails and push notifications for Couchsurfing events, click the upside-down triangle (top right corner of any page, to the right of your profile picture on the Couchsurfing nav bar; Screenshot 14-34). Click "Account & Settings" on the drop-down menu. On the "Account & Settings" page, click "Emails & Push Notifications" (left-hand side menu; Screenshot 14-35). Select the updates you want to receive and how you want to receive them (Email or Push) by making selections under "Email & Push Communications" (Screenshot 14-36). Click the "Save Changes" button at the bottom of the page to save your selections.

Idea #312: Know How to Get More Help With Couchsurfing Events

To get more help with Couchsurfing events, access the Couchsurfing "Help Center."

1. Go to the website:
    https://support.Couchsurfing.org

    OR:

2. Click "*Support*" on the bottom nav menu (located on any Couchsurfing page).

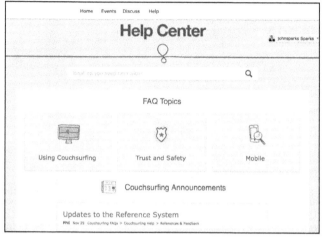

Screenshot 14-37

Go to: https://support.Couchsurfing.org or click "Support" on the bottom nav menu (located on any Couchsurfing page).

PART 15

Surf Electrifying Events with the Couchsurfing App

 Idea #313: Know How to Use The Couchsurfing App to Start Searching for Events in Your Home Location

---

▲ Click the *"Couchsurfing"* button 🌐 (bottom menu bar) to go to the Couchsurfing Dashboard.

▲ Scroll down the Couchsurfing Dashboard and locate the section heading *"What's Happening Nearby?"*

✦ A listing of events happening near your location appears here.

▲ Click any event to go to the event detail page for that event.

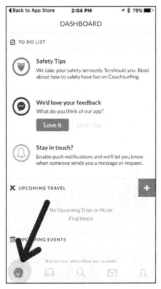

Screenshot 15-1   Screenshot 15-2

Screenshot 15-3

To view events in your area using the Couchsurfing app, click the "Couchsurfing" button (bottom menu bar; Screenshot 15-1) to go to the Couchsurfing Dashboard. Scroll down the Couchsurfing Dashboard (Screenshot 15-2) and locate the section heading "What's Happening Nearby?" (Screenshot 15-3). A listing of events happening near your location will appear here. Click any event to go to the event detail page for that event.

Idea #314: Understand How to Use the Couchsurfing App to Search and View Events in Other Cities

1. Click the *"Search"* button 🔍 (bottom menu bar).

2. On the search page, click the search bar at the top of the screen

3. After clicking the search bar, click the *"Event"* tab 📅 (upper right of the screen).
   Event

4. Type in the name of the city you want to view events for.

Screenshot 15-4

Screenshot 15-5

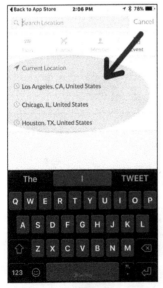

Screenshot 15-6

Screenshot 15-7

To view and RSVP for events in other cities, click the "Search" button (bottom menu bar; Screenshot 15-4). On the search page, click the search bar at the top of the screen. After clicking the search bar, click the "Event" tab (upper right of the screen; Screenshot 15-5). Type in the name of the city you want to view events for and click the name of the city on the drop-down menu (Screenshot 15-6). The event listings page for the location of your choice will appear (Screenshot 15-7).

 ## Idea #315: Understand an Alternate Way to Search and View Events in Other Cities

▲ If you haven't RSVP'd for any events, you can search for events by clicking *"Search for Events"* (located on the Couchsurfing Dashboard under the *"Upcoming Events"* section heading).

▲ Once you have RSVP'd for an event *"Search for Events"* is replaced with an event listing you are going to.

▲ To find events to attend after you have RSVP'd for an event:

✦ Look at the event listings under the section heading: *"What's Happening Nearby?"* (located on the Couchsurfing Dashboard).

✦ Clicking the *"Search"* button 🔍 (bottom menu bar) and follow the steps in Idea #314.

▲ Since *"Search for Events"* doesn't always
appear on the Couchsurfing Dashboard,
the easiest way to search for events might
be using the *"Search"* button located on the
bottom menu bar.

Screenshot 15-8

Screenshot 15-9

*If you haven't RSVP'd for any events on Couchsurfing, you
can search for events by clicking "Search for Events" (on the
Couchsurfing Dashboard under the "Upcoming Events" section
heading; Screenshot 15-8). Once you have RSVP'd for an event,
"Search for Events" will no longer appear on the dashboard
(Screenshot 15-9). Since "Search for Events" doesn't always
appear on the Couchsurfing Dashboard, the easiest way to
search for events might be using the "Search" button located on
the bottom menu bar.*

Idea #316: Understand What You Can Find on an Event Detail Page on the Couchsurfing App

▲ Click any event on an event listings page to go to the event detail page for that event.

▲ On the event detail page, you will find the following:

   ✦ Name of the event

   ✦ *"Join"* button to RSVP for the event

   ✦ *"Invite"* button to invite others to attend the event via SMS (text message)

   ✦ Address of the event

   ✦ Date of the event

   ✦ List of *"Attendees"* going to the event

   ✦ List of *"Organizers"* hosting the event

   ✦ Description of the event

   ✦ Map of the event venue

   ✦ *Share icon* 📤 to share the event on social media

   ✦ Event discussion board to post public comments

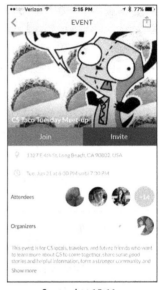

| Screenshot 15-10 | Screenshot 15-11 |

Click any event on an event listings page (Screenshot 15-10) to go to an event detail page for that event (Screenshot 15-11).

Idea #317: Know How to Use the Couchsurfing App to RSVP for Couchsurfing Events

▲ To RSVP for a Couchsurfing event on the Couchsurfing app, click the "*Join*" button on any event detail page.

▲ Once you click the "Join" button, the following will happen:

- *"You joined this event"* will appear briefly at the bottom of the screen on the event detail page.

- The *"Join"* button will change to "Going" on the event detail page.

- Your name will appear with the other event *"Attendees"* on the event detail page.

- The event will appear under the section heading for *"Upcoming Events"* on the Couchsurfing Dashboard.

- The event will appear on the *"My Events"* page (See Idea #315).

- The event organizer will receive a notification that you plan to attend the event.

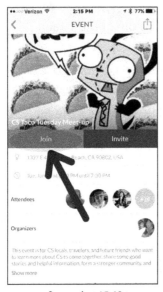

Screenshot 15-12

Screenshot 15-13

Screenshot 15-14

Click the "Join" button on any event detail page to RSVP for an event (Screenshot 15-12). The "Join" button will change to "Going," and "You joined this event" will appear briefly at the bottom of the screen (Screenshot 15-13). The event will appear under the section heading for "Upcoming Events" on the Couchsurfing Dashboard (Screenshot 15-14).

Idea #318: Understand How to Add a Couchsurfing Event to Your Calendar Using the Couchsurfing App

At the current time, the Couchsurfing app does not have the "add to calendar" feature for individual Couchsurfing events. However, if you sync your Couchsurfing activity with your calendar using the web-based version, any events you join on the app will still appear on your calendar.

See Idea #298 for details on synching your Couchsurfing activity with your calendar using the web-based version.

Idea #319: Use Apple Maps to Locate and Get Directions to Couchsurfing Events

▲ Go to any event detail page (See Idea #316).

▲ Click the address of the event (underneath the *"Going/Invite"* buttons).

▲ A pop-up menu will appear (bottom of the screen).

▲ Click *"Open in Apple Maps."*

▲ Apple Maps will launch. A map showing the event location will be displayed.

▲ Click the *car position indicator* on the map to get driving directions.

You can also access Apple Maps by clicking the map on any event detail page. After clicking the map, a larger map will appear. Select *"Open Maps App"* (top right corner of the screen). A pop-up menu will appear. Click *"Open in Apple Maps."*

Screenshot 15-15

Screenshot 15-16

Screenshot 15-17

To locate/get directions to a Couchsurfing event using Apple Maps, go to any event detail page and click the address of the event (underneath the "Going/Invite" buttons; Screenshot 15-15). A pop-up menu will appear. Click "Open in Apple Maps" (Screenshot 15-16). Apple Maps will launch. A map showing the event location will be displayed (Screenshot 15-17). Click the car position indicator on the map to get driving directions.

Idea #320: Use Google Maps to Locate and Get Directions to Couchsurfing Events

- ▲ Go to any event detail page (See Idea #316).

- ▲ Click the address of the event (underneath the *"Going/Invite"* buttons).

- ▲ A pop-up menu will appear (bottom of the screen).

- ▲ Click *"Cancel"* on the pop-up menu.

- ▲ A pop-up box will appear (center of the screen) that says *"Couchsurfing wants to open Google Maps."*

- ▲ Click *"Open"* on the pop-up box.

- ▲ Google Maps will launch and a map showing the event location will be displayed.

- ▲ Select *"Open"* when the pop-up box appears that says *"Couchsurfing wants to open Google Maps."*

You can also access Google Maps by clicking the map on any event detail page. After clicking the map, a larger map will appear. Select *"Open Maps App"* (top right corner of the screen). A pop-up menu will appear. Click *"Cancel"* on the pop-up menu and follow the prompts.

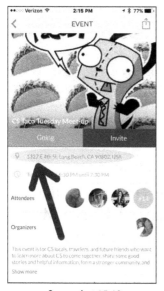

Screenshot 15-18

Screenshot 15-19

Screenshot 15-20

Screenshot 15-21

To locate/get directions to a Couchsurfing event using Google Maps, go to any event detail page and click the address of the event (underneath the "Going/Invite" buttons; Screenshot 15-18). A pop-up menu will appear. Click "Cancel" on the pop-up menu (Screenshot 15-19). A pop-up box will appear (center of the screen; Screenshot 15-20) that says "Couchsurfing wants to open Google Maps". Click "Open" on the pop-up box. Google Maps will launch. A map showing the event location will be displayed (Screenshot 15-21).

Idea #321: Know How to Use the Couchsurfing App to Discover More Details About Who Organized a Couchsurfing Event

▲ Go to any event detail page (See Idea #316).

▲ Click *"Organizers"* (middle of the page).

▲ On the next page, you will see a listing of all the organizers of the event.

▲ Click the organizer's name to go to their Couchsurfing profile page.

    ✦ Similar to the web-based version, on the Couchsurfing app you will be able to view the following:

        • Age

        • Current location

        • Occupation

        • Education

- Interests
- Hometown
- References
- Languages spoken
- What they use Couchsurfing for
- Couchsurfing groups they belong to
- How long they've been on Couchsurfing
- Whether or not they're a verified Couchsurfing user
- If they're accepting Couchsurfing guests at their home

Screenshot 15-22

Screenshot 15-23

Screenshot 15-24

Click "Organizers" on any event detail page to see a listing of all the organizers of an event (Screenshot 15-22). Click the name of an event organizer (Screenshot 15-23) to view the organizer's profile page (Screenshot 15-24).

Idea #322: Know How to Use the Couchsurfing App to Contact the Organizer of a Couchsurfing Event

▲ Go to any event organizer's profile page (See Idea #321).

▲ Click the *"Message"* button 🖂

▲ A new page will appear that will allow you
to type and send a message to the event
organizer.

Screenshot 15-25

Screenshot 15-26

*Click the "Message" button on an organizer's profile page
(Screenshot 15-25) to send the organizer of a Couchsurfing event
a message. A new page will appear that will allow you to type and
send a message to the event organizer (Screenshot 15-26).*

Idea #323: Know How to Leave a Reference Using the Couchsurfing App

▲ Click the menu button represented by three dots ⬚⋯ (upper right corner of the screen) on any event organizer or attendee's profile page.

▲ A pop-up menu will appear (bottom of the screen).

▲ Click "*Write Reference*" on the pop-up menu.

▲ On the personal reference page, choose from:

✦ "*Yes, I'd recommend*"

✦ "*No, I wouldn't recommend*"

▲ Leave a comment in the section that says "*What was your experience with…*"

▲ Click "*Submit Reference.*"

Screenshot 15-27

Screenshot 15-28

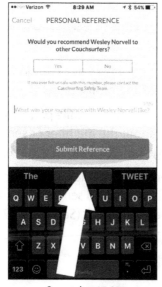

Screenshot 15-29

To write a reference on the Couchsurfing app, click the menu button represented by three dots (upper right corner of the screen) on any event organizer or attendee's profile page (Screenshot 15-27). A pop-up menu will appear (bottom of the screen). Click "Write Reference" on the pop-up menu (Screenshot 15-28). On the personal reference page, choose from: "Yes, I'd Recommend" or "No, I wouldn't recommend" and leave a comment. Click "Submit Reference" (Screenshot 15-29).

Idea #324: Know How to Use the Couchsurfing App to View Attendees Going to an Event and Send Them a Message

1. Go to any event detail page (See Idea #316).

2. Click *"Attendees"* (top of the page).

3. On the next page, you will see a listing of all the attendees of the event.

4. Click an attendee's name to go to their Couchsurfing profile page.

5. On the member's profile page, view details about the member or send them a message before going to the event.

   ✦ Send the attendee a message the same way you would send a message to an event organizer (See Idea #322).

Screenshot 15-30

Screenshot 15-31

Screenshot 15-32

*Click "Attendees" on any event detail page (Screenshot 15-30) to
see a listing of all the attendees of an event. Click the name of an
attendee (Screenshot 15-31) to view the attendee's profile page
(Screenshot 15-32).*

Idea #325: Know How to Use the Couchsurfing App to Invite Other Friends via SMS to a Couchsurfing Event

▲ Go to any event detail page (See Idea #316).

▲ Click the *"Invite"* button (underneath the event photo).

▲ A pop-up menu will appear (bottom of the screen).

▲ Click *"SMS"* (text message) on the pop-up menu.

▲ Enter a name from your contact list in the *"To:"* field and send them a link to the event as a text message.

Screenshot 15-33

Screenshot 15-34

Screenshot 15-35

Select the "Invite" button to invite other Couchsurfing friends with an event (underneath the event photo; Screenshot 15-33). A pop-up menu will appear (bottom of the screen). Click "SMS" (text message) on the pop-up menu (Screenshot 15-34). Enter a name from your contact list in the "To:" field, and send them a link to the event as a text message (Screenshot 15-35).

Idea #326: Know How to Share an Event on the Couchsurfing App with Other Social Media Sites

▲ Go to the event detail page for any event (See Idea #316).

▲ Click the *share icon* ⬆️ (upper right corner of the screen).

▲ A pop-up menu will appear (bottom of the screen).

▲ Share the event via email, SMS (text message), AirDrop, or any of the listed social media platforms.

✦ You can also add the page to your reading list (so you can go back to it later), or select *"Copy"* to save the page link to your clipboard.

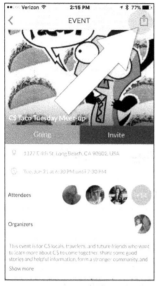

Screenshot 15-36   *Screenshot 15-37*

To share an event, click the share icon (upper right corner of the screen; Screenshot 15-36). A pop-up menu will appear (bottom of the screen). Share the event via email, SMS (text message), AirDrop, or any of the listed social media platforms. (Screenshot 15-37).

 ## Idea #327: Know How to Cancel Your RSVP for a Couchsurfing Event Using the Couchsurfing App

▲ Go to the event detail page for any event (See Idea #316).

▲ Click and hold the green button that says *"Going"* (underneath the event photo).

▲ A pop-up menu will appear (bottom of the screen).

▲ Click *"Leave."*

 ✦ The green button that says "*Going*" will be replaced with a blue button that says "*Join.*"

 ✦ The event will no longer appear on the Couchsurfing Dashboard under *"My Upcoming Events."*

 ✦ The organizer will be notified you are not attending.

Screenshot 15-38   *Screenshot 15-39*

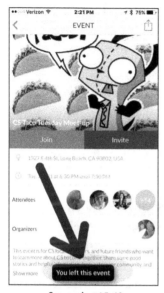

Screenshot 15-40   Screenshot 15-41

To cancel your RSVP to a Couchsurfing event, click and hold the green button that says "Going" (underneath the event photo; Screenshot 15-38). A pop-up menu will appear (bottom of the screen). Click "Leave". (Screenshot 15-39). The green "Going" button will change back to "Join," and "You left this event" will appear briefly at the bottom of the screen (Screenshot 15-40). The event will no longer appear under the section heading "Upcoming Events" on the Couchsurfing Dashboard (Screenshot 15-41).

Idea #328: Understand How to Create New Events on the Couchsurfing App

▲ At the time of this book's publication, Couchsurfing does not support the ability to create new events on its app.

▲ See Idea #310 to create an event on the web-based version of Couchsurfing.com

 ## Idea #329: Understand How to Change/Adjust Emails and Push Notifications for Events on the Couchsurfing App

1. Click the *profile button* ♌ (bottom right corner on the bottom menu bar).

2. The Couchsurfing "*Account*" page will appear.

3. Click *"Notification Settings"* on the Couchsurfing "*Account*" page

4. Scroll down to the section heading that says "*Events*."

5. Select the updates you want to receive and how you want to receive them (Email or Push).

Screenshot 15-42

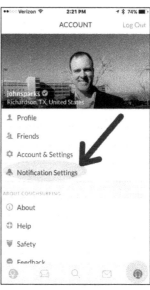

Screenshot 15-43

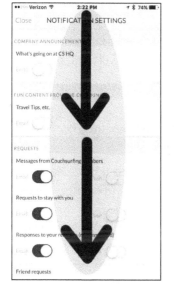

Screenshot 15-44

Screenshot 15-45

To change/adjust emails and push notifications for events on the Couchsurfing app, click the profile button(bottom right corner on the bottom menu bar; Screenshot 15-42). The Couchsurfing "Account" page will appear. Click "Notification Settings" on the "Account" page (Screenshot 15-43). Scroll down to the section that says "Events." (Screenshot 15-44). Select the updates you want to receive and how you want to receive them (Screenshot 15-45).

Idea #330: Know How to Get More Help with Couchsurfing Events on the Couchsurfing App

1. Click the profile button 𝛺 (bottom right corner, on the bottom menu bar).

   ✦ The Couchsurfing "*Account*" page will appear.

2. Click "*Help*" on the Couchsurfing "*Account*" page.

   ✦ The device web browser will launch.

   ✦ The Couchsurfing "*Help Center*" will appear.

3. Type the word "*Events*" in the search box on the "*Help Center*" page.

4. Next, click the *search icon* to get more help and support with Couchsurfing events.

Screenshot 15-46

Screenshot 15-47

Screenshot 15-48

To get more help with Couchsurfing events, access the Couchsurfing "Help Center" through the Couchsurfing app. Click the profile button (bottom right corner on the bottom menu bar; Screenshot 15-46). The Couchsurfing "Account" page will appear. Click "Help" on the Couchsurfing "Account" page (Screenshot 15-47). The Couchsurfing "Help Center" will appear (Screenshot 15-48). Type the word "Events" in the search box on the "Help Center" page. Next, click the search icon to get more help and support with Couchsurfing events.

PART 16
Become a World-Class Network Marketer

 Idea #331: Check for Events on Other Popular Event Apps and Websites

- ▲ In this book, we took an in-depth look at six of the most popular event sites: Meetup, Eventbrite, Facebook, Yelp, Google+, and Couchsurfing.

- ▲ To be a world-class marketer, these aren't the only websites and apps you should use to find events. Check out these others:

  - ✦ **All Events in City:**

    With this app, you never have to be worried about being bored again! All

Events in City has 32 million events across more than 30,000 cities.

- **Website:** https://allevents.in
- **iPhone All Events App:**

  https://itunes.apple.com/ us/app/all-events-in-city/ id488116646?mt=8

- **Android All Events App:**

  https://play.google.com/store/ apps/details?id=com.amitech. allevents

✦ **Eventbase:**

Specializes in festivals, conferences, trade shows, and fairs. Sort events by date, distance, and also alphabetically.

- **Website:** https://eventbase.com/

✦ **Gravy:**

What kind of mood are you in? Are you feeling lively, classy, brainy, or like its playtime? Gravy shows you the most relevant event ideas based on your mood.

- **Website:** http://findgravy.com
- **iPhone Gravy App:**

  https://itunes.apple.com/us/app/ gravy-fun-things-to-do-nearby/ id509336320?mt=8

- **Android Gravy App:**

    https://play.google.com/
    store/apps/details?id=com.
    timeRAZOR&hl=en

 ## Idea #332: Do Not Limit Yourself to Locating Networking Events Through Websites and Apps

Explore every resource and opportunity that is available. Consider checking out:

▲ *Word of mouth events:* Sometimes word of mouth events are the best to attend. Just show up!

▲ *Local chambers of commerce:* Make a list of chambers of commerce near you and contact them. Attend lunch and learn activities, workshops, and power networking groups.

▲ *Churches:* Churches are great places to find events. Many churches offer:

   ✦ Community groups/small groups

   ✦ Job clubs and ministries for people out of work.

▲ *Alumni Clubs:* Check with the university you graduated from to see what types of events they host nearby.

▲ *Volunteering:* Locate individuals, businesses, and non-profits who are looking for assistance and offer to lend a helping hand.

 ## Idea #333: Understand That the Power of Social Media Is Centered around Real-Life Networking

▲ *Online* and *offline:* It's important to be networking both online and offline simultaneously.

▲ Real-life networking will enhance the online experience. The online experience will also enhance real-life networking.

▲ The same way you conduct real-life networking is how you should manage personal brands online.

▲ *Remember,* a successful personal brand is key to getting people interested in a business brand.

Idea #334: Show up Early to Networking Events

▲ When you attend networking events, be sure to be one of the first ones there.

▲ The speakers and organizers arrive early and they are important people to meet.

▲ Pitch in to help set up before a networking event, or stay after and help clean up. You will learn a lot about the group and its members by volunteering.

▲ When you look for ways to help the group, group leaders will look for ways to help you. Group leaders have invaluable resources to offer both during and after an event is over.

 Idea #335: Be Prepared for the Unexpected

Expect that no matter how much you plan, the unexpected will always happen when trying to locate a networking event you have never been to before. For example, even with the best GPS, you can easily end up driving around in circles. Leave early and allow plenty of extra time to stop and ask for directions.

Idea #336: Build a Fan Base of Offline Supporters at Networking Events

▲ Intentionally seek out offline supporters who believe in you.

✦ On days you need to spend time online, offline supporters become the eyes and ears for what you missed at networking groups.

✦ Hopefully your offline supporters will speak highly of you in your absence at networking groups during the group's announcements, thank you's, and recognitions.

▲ Take time to thank offline supporters publicly and privately when you see them.

Remember, hearing a recommendation coming from someone else is more credible than anything you could say about yourself and your abilities.

Idea #337: Be Present and Get Your Face out of Your Technology at Networking Events

▲ Be mindful about technology at networking events. If you are concerned the technology is going to be too distracting, leave it in the car.

▲ Some networking events have strict policies prohibiting technology. Even If they don't, make it your personal policy to be fully present.

▲ Put your phone on vibrate. Refrain from monitoring emails, text messages, or surfing the web and other apps during meetings.

▲ If you receive a phone call, or even a text message, leave the room to respond.

▲ While at a networking event, keep 100% of the focus and attention on the others at the meeting.

 Idea #338: Learn How to Shake Hands in a Way That Endears Yourself to Others

When shaking hands, lightly tap on the other person's pulse point with your index finger one time.

▲ Some experts believe that an ever-so-slight and discreet tap will send the person you are greeting some positive energy.

Idea #339: Track the Networking Groups That Friends and Competitors Are Going To

Keep tabs on competitors and the events they are attending via social media. Worthwhile business opportunities might exist at networking groups your competitors are attending. You might want to consider attending these events and be known in these circles as well.

- ▲ When you see a competitor has posted on social media about an event they have attended, do the following:
    - ✦ Log the event on a spreadsheet.
        - • On the spreadsheet, include the competitor's name, the name of the event, date(s) of the event, event location, and website URL for the event.
    - ✦ Reach out to the organizer of the event.
        - • Let the organizer know that you would be interested in participating.
    - ✦ Make plans to attend the event.

You want to be top of mind when others think of people they know in your industry.

Idea #340: Bring Products to the Events and Ask for the Sale

Savvy networkers have their products with them at all the networking events they attend. They use each networking opportunity to talk about their products.

▲ For items such as jewelry and books, hold them up and pass them around during your 30-second introduction. This way other networkers can see your products, touch them, and want to buy them when you are at the events.

 ## Idea #341: Get a Credit Card Reader to Bring to Networking Events

▲ Bring a credit card reader with you to networking groups so you can make a quick sell and accept payment on the spot.

Popular mobile credit card readers include:

▲ **Square:**
https://squareup.com/reader

▲ **PayPal Here:**
https://paypal.com/here

▲ **Pay Anywhere:**
http://www.payanywhere.com

▲ **Intuit QuickBooks Payments:**
http://payments.intuit.com

▲ **Check out reviews for each at:**
http://credit-card-processing-review
.toptenreviews.com/mobile-credit-card
-processing/flint-review.html

 ### Idea #342: Reach out to the Organizers Before You Attend Their Event

Reach out to the event organizers of a networking group before attending their events to:

▲ Make sure the group is still meeting.

▲ Confirm the meeting times and location.

▲ Find out the format of the group.

✦ You'll need to know if you'll have the opportunity to give your 30-second introduction.

▲ Find out how many people typically attend the group.

▲ Ask about the group's joining requirements, policies and procedures.

▲ Find out of the group is an open group or a closed group.

✦ Open groups allow anyone to join.

✦ Closed groups only allow one person from each industry to join.

✦ Ask if members can sell their products at the meetings.

▲ Find out if you have to be a member of the group before you can be a featured speaker at the group.

▲ Ask how long the group has been around.

✦ Groups that have been around shorter amounts of time may be more lenient on their joining requirements.

▲ Confirm the cost of any meeting dues and/ or meeting fees.

 ## Idea #343: Put Networking Groups on Your Fixed Calendar

▲ It's important to find at least one or two networking groups that you enjoy attending.

▲ Put these groups on your fixed calendar, and make it a point to attend each and every meeting. Don't be absent!

✦ If business drops, you don't want to have to ask yourself what you were doing six months prior to prospect for new clients.

Idea #344: Understand Why the Best Networking Events to Attend Are Not Necessarily the Most Expensive Networking Events to Attend

▲ Members who pay higher entrance fees or parking fees to attend networking meetings may be more reluctant to support the products and services others have to offer once inside the meeting.

▲ Attendees at meetings with lower entrance fees might be willing to spend extra money on products and services.

Idea #345: Start a Spreadsheet of the Meeting Fees You Pay

▲ Even though some networking meetings might cost one or two dollars, it can add up quickly.

　✦ Using a spreadsheet makes it easier to claim your networking meetings as business expenses on your taxes at the end of the year.

Idea #346: Donate Products and Services to Group Organizers for a Weekly Raffle or Drawing

▲ Offer a sample product or your services to the organizers of a networking group you attend to give away as a door prize.

  ✦ Before the drawing, the organizer will thank you publicly for donating the prize.

  ✦ The person who wins the prize will share it with others at the event.

  ✦ This creates buzz and attendees won't want to leave the event until they find out more about your product or service.

 Idea #347: Introduce Yourself to the Group Organizers, Co-Organizers, Influencers/Leaders, and Speakers at a Group

▲ A group's organizers and co-organizers are important, but so are those who are seen as influencers or leaders inside the group.

  ✦ Learn which attendees are influencers in the group and go out of the way to meet them.

- ✦ Be sure to introduce yourself to the speaker before or after the event.

    - Speakers not only have relationships with organizers at the group you're at but also at other groups you might want to attend.

    - Speakers can provide good leads and referrals.

Idea #348: Get a List of All the Attendees at the Meeting

▲ Some of the meetings may provide a list of names and contact information to guests and visitors in attendance.

▲ On these lists, you'll find the names and contact information for the organizers, members, and guests/visitors of the group.

- ✦ Do your best to get a copy of this list before the meeting starts. Having it beforehand will allow you to:

    - Jot down meeting notes next to an attendee's name during their 30-second introduction.

    - Plan who you want to speak to when the meeting ends before attendees start to leave.

▲ Even if the list only shows attendees from the previous meeting, still go ahead and pick one up.

  ✦ Make note of attendees on the list who are present this time versus last time.

    • This will give you some indication if the group is a transient group or if people return week after week.

▲ If you don't see a list of attendees, ask the group organizer for one.

  ✦ Some organizers will email a list of attendees to everyone once the meeting is over.

PART 17

Remember:
Fortune Is in the Follow-Up

 Idea #349: Understand Why You Should Follow up With People After A Networking Event

---

▲ Following up after a meeting shows people you are interested in getting to know them.

▲ The goal of following up with people should be to work on setting up a one-to-one meeting to learn more about each other.

▲ Make it a priority to understand what people do, not what you "think" they do after brief encounters with them at networking groups.

Idea #350: Do More Research on Attendees, Organizers, and Speakers Before and After the Meetings

▲ Research attendees, organizers, and speakers before and after a meeting to locate common threads.

▲ Look at attendees, organizers, and speakers' profiles on LinkedIn.

✦ You may find other connecting points or interests.

Idea #351: Understand How to Follow up With Those You Meet at a Networking Event

▲ How did the attendees at a networking event say they prefer you to make contact with them?

✦ Did you ask them outright, or did they give you any clues during your conversation? Reach out to people the way they want you to reach out to them.

Idea #352: Become Better at Following up With People by Phone

1. When someone answers their phone:

    ✦ Remind the person who you are.

    ✦ Regardless if the call is a scheduled call or not, ask the person if it's still a good time to talk.

2. When leaving a voicemail:

    ✦ Give your name.

    ✦ State your phone number twice and be sure to say it slowly. Leave your phone number regardless if you think the person already has it.

    ✦ Remind the person when and where you met them.

    ✦ State the purpose of your call.

    ✦ Leave your name again at the end of the message.

3. When text messaging:

    ✦ After leaving a voicemail message, immediately follow up with a text message.

    ✦ Whenever possible, send a text message instead of sending an email.

        • Text messages have an 80% read rate compared to email which has a 20% read rate.

✦   Be sure to include your first and last name in the text message so the person will know who sent it.

Idea #353: Strike While the Iron Is Hot and Invite Those You Meet to Connect on Social Media

▲   Do not wait to connect with people on social media.

✦   Send a connection request on social media within 48 hours of meeting someone offline.

✦   People who meet new people every day and attend several networking groups a week may not remember you two days from now.

▲   The best place to connect with business professionals whom you meet for the very first time is on LinkedIn.

Idea #354: Send Others You Meet at Networking Groups a First-Class Thank You Note

▲   Send a handwritten thank you note.

✦   In the age of email and texts, a handwritten thank you note always stands out.

- ✦ Send a personalized thank you note to the organizers and speakers you meet at an event.

- ✦ Thank anyone who offered to help you in any way, even if they haven't done it yet. Your note will serve as a reminder.

▲ Write thank you notes using a blue, rollerball pen.

- ✦ Blue is the color of teamwork.

  - It stands for compassion, honesty, and sincerity.

- ✦ The color black can come across as intimidating and has an authoritarian tone.

- ✦ Rollerballs use water-based gels, or liquid ink and have a bold appearance.

▲ Understand how the "*3-3-3 Rule*" works for thank you notes:

- ✦ Keep the thank you note <u>three</u> sentences long.

- ✦ Make sure the person receives the thank you note within <u>three</u> days after you meet them.

- ✦ Follow up with a phone call <u>three</u> days after you think the note was received.

Idea #355: Start Scheduling One-To-Ones Right Away

▲ Ask those you speak with during follow-up conversations to do a one-to-one with you.

▲ Focus on relationships.

▲ Practice good eye contact.

✦ Remember, the eyes are the windows to the soul.

✦ This meeting is about building trust and reaching people on another level.

▲ Ask people you meet how you can help them.

▲ Listen, Listen, Listen!

PART 18

Take Risks and Watch the Pieces Fall into Place!

 Idea #356: Just Say "Yes" to Every Opportunity!

▲ Always say "Yes" when someone asks you for help either before, during, or after an event.

▲ Be willing to take on any and all new projects.

▲ You don't want a "No" to end any future opportunities with that individual.

Idea #357:
Meet 5 New People Every Day

▲ Make it a goal to meet five new people, face-to-face, every day.

✦ Have conversations with these five new people.

• The conversations don't have to be long ones.

• Sometimes you'll find that these conversations are the stepping stones to a business relationship down the line.

 Idea #358:
Learn 10 New Things Every Day

▲ Take the challenge to learn ten new things every day.

✦ It helps to know a little bit about everything when networking and relating to others.

• Strive to have more areas of knowledge outside of your career, hobbies, and interests.

• Keep up with current events.

+ Develop a broader understanding of the world around you.

  • Being a well-rounded person is an ongoing process.

Idea #359: Never Stop Improving and Reinventing Yourself

Do not stop improving—do not stop reinventing yourself.

▲ Periodically check your branding to ensure you're current with industry standards.

▲ Look for new opportunities for professional development.

When meeting others at networking groups, have the attitude that while you might continue to look the same on the outside, everything about you is continuing to grow and improve on the inside.

Idea #360: Rotate the Networking Groups You Visit

▲ Go to groups where people know little about the subject matter that you know most about.

✦ Groups catering specifically to your industry or niche may not be the best groups to attend.

- Frequently, people at groups catering to your niche will look at others in the niche as competition and won't help them.

- Some people at groups catering to your niche will appear to have a "know-it-all" attitude.

- While it's important to go to these groups, do so on a less frequent basis.

  ✧ Roughly 80% of the groups you attend should be outside your industry. 20% of the groups you attend should be inside your industry.

Idea #361: Remember That Attitude and Persistence Are Key in Networking!

▲ Don't forget when you're networking that it's easier to steer a moving car than one sitting still.

▲ Moving forward a little bit in building relationships is better than not moving forward at all.

- ▲ Networking takes time and relationships are hard work.

- ▲ Those who have a great attitude, are persistent, and who don't give up will see the most success when it's all said and done.

Idea #362: Think Positive When You're Networking!

- ▲ Think positive when you're networking. When you least expect it, something great will come along—something better than you ever anticipated.

- ▲ Remember that in life it sometimes takes courage to achieve your goals.

- ▲ If you want something to happen, you must try new things and have faith.

Idea #363: Practice Good Ethics at Networking Events and in Life

- ▲ *"Your online brand is as important as your offline brand activities."*

- ▲ Read this Facebook post on practicing good ethics at events by internationally recognized branding coach, Bernard Kelvin Clive:

Bernard Kelvin Clive
35 mins ·

Event Ethics for #SocialMedia Lovers

1. Know your role: If you are not the official photographer, don't distract others. Don't run around taking pictures of every moment. [We know you have a cool iPad, Techno Phone, China Phone, etc., but hey you are not the photographer].

2. Don't be the first to break the news (especially the mishaps), you are not the MC, announcer or broadcaster. You are a guest, if you are not having a good time, at best leave or sit quietly. Note: it's not about you, stop whining and tweeting about it.

3. Don't be the celebrity stalker: rushing to take pictures with the 'famed' so you can share on social media. [They may not even remember you, LOL]

4. "Do you know who I am" status, you don't go assuming everyone should know you, because you are the popular face on TV, voice on radio or Facebook guru. Yes, people may or may not make you out, so relax your ego and enjoy the event, either recognized or not. Maintain a low profile; it's not a celebrity hangout. The focus is on the event not you; don't try to steal the show.

5. Just be nice to people, you may not know who would be watching and following you on social media. NB: You online brand is as important as your offline brand activities.

Screenshot 18-1

Event Ethics from Bernard Kelvin Clive as shared on Facebook (used by permission).

▲   To listen to Kelvin Clive's podcast on event ethics, go to http://bit.ly/EventEthics

 ### Idea #364: Understand That the Individuals Having Success at Networking Today Are Those Who Are Authentic

▲   In this day where everything is automated, the individuals who are most successful at networking are the ones that come across as "real people."

  ✦   Anything you can do to add your own personal touch to a relationship, do it!

  ✦   Excellence is created by reaching out, following up, and keeping everything genuine and personal.

 ### Idea #365: NEVER Burn Bridges!

Finally, always remember that it's not *what* we have in life. Instead, it's *who* we have in our life that matter. Things can be replaced, but people cannot. Need we say else?? ☺☺

APPENDIX 1
Marketing and SEO Resources

Domain Registration:

▲ GoDaddy

https://www.godaddy.com

▲ BlueHost

https://www.bluehost.com/cgi-bin/
signup?domain_only=1

▲ HostGator

https://register.hostgator.com

Top 10 Business Directories to Be Listed in for Local Marketing:

1. Google Local Places
2. Yelp for Business Owners
3. Bing Places for Business
4. Merchant Circle
5. Local.com
6. Expressupdate.com
7. Yext and MapQuest
8. Insiderpages.com
9. Foursquare for Business
10. Abaco Small Business from Yahoo (Formerly Yahoo Small Business)

Listings of Local Search Directories:

▲ Top 10 Free USA Local Business Directory Sites List 2016-2017

http://www.ads2020.marketing/2014/02/ 10-free-usa-local-business-sites-2014.html

▲ Top 20 Local Business Directories You Need to Be On

http://localvox.com/blog/top-local -business-directories/

▲ The Ultimate List: 50 Online Local Business Directories

http://blog.hubspot.com/blog/tabid/
6307/bid/10322/The-Ultimate-List
-50-Local-Business-Directories.aspx
-sm.000018xkhd737ne1xvwdopuoq5qhi

▲ Top 15 Local Directory Listing Services

http://www.practicalecommerce.com/
articles/115895-top-15-local-directory
-listing-services

▲ Top 50 Local Citation Sites – US, UK,
Canada and Australia

https://www.brightlocal.com/2013/09/11/
top-50-local-citation-sites/

Branding:

▲ Securing Your Online Brand and
Domain/Username Search:

Namechk.com
https://namechk.com

▲ Business Card Printing and Marketing
Materials:

Vistaprint
http://www.vistaprint.com

▲ Support with Business Cards and Graphics:

Vistaprint Customer Service
1-866-614-8002

▲ CamCard Business Card Scanner:

CamCard App for iPhone
https://itunes.apple.com/us/app/camcard
-free-business-card/id355472887?mt=8

CamCard App for Android
https://play.google.com/store/apps/
details?id=com.intsig.BCRLite&hl=en

▲ Listings of Business Card Scanners:

iPhone Business Card Scanner Apps
http://www.igeeksblog.com/best-business
-card-reader-scanner-apps-for-iphone/

Android Business Card Scanner Apps
http://www.androidheadlines.
com/2015/01/featured-top-10-business
-card-scanner-apps-android.html

More iPhone and Android Business Card
Scanner Apps
http://www.scrubly.com/blog/tech-tips/
5-great-business-card-apps-smartphone/

▲ Creating Vocal Executive Presence:

Want to Sound Like a Leader? Start by
Saying Your Name Right

[VIDEO] Dr. Laura Sicola, Vocal Impact
Specialist

http://bit.ly/SayUrName

▲ Ethics for Social Media Lovers at Events:

[PODCAST] Bernard Kelvin Clive, Internationally Recognized Lifestyle Entrepreneur, Personal Branding Coach, Brand Strategist

http://bit.ly/EventEthics

APPENDIX 2
Event Websites, Apps, and Resources

▲   All Events In City:
    https://allevents.in

    iPhone All Events App:
    https://itunes.apple.com/us/app/all
    -events-in-city/id488116646?mt=8

    Android All Events App:
    https://play.google.com/store/apps/
    details?id=com.amitech.allevents

▲   Couchsurfing:
    https://www.Couchsurfing.com

    iPhone Couchsurfing App:
    https://itunes.apple.com/us/
    app/Couchsurfing-travel-app/
    id525642917?mt=8

Android Couchsurfing App:
https://play.google.com/store/apps/
details?id=com.couchsurfing.mobile.
android&hl=en

Couchsurfing Help Center:
https://support.Couchsurfing.org

Couchsurfing Help Center (Mobile App):

1. Click the profile button ♙ (bottom
    right corner, on the bottom menu bar).

    •   The Couchsurfing "*Account*" page
        will appear.

2. Click "*Help*" on the Couchsurfing
    "*Account*" page.

    •   The device web browser will
        launch.

    •   The Couchsurfing "*Help Center*" will
        appear.

▲ Eventbase:
  https://eventbase.com/

▲ Eventbrite:
  https://www.eventbrite.com

  iPhone Eventbrite App:
  https://itunes.apple.com/us/
  app/eventbrite-local-events-fun/
  id487922291?mt=8

Android Eventbrite App:
https://play.google.com/store/apps/
details?id=com.eventbrite.attendee&hl=en

Eventbrite Support:
https://www.eventbrite.com/support

Eventbrite Support (Mobile App):

✦ Click the "*Me*" button 🧍 (bottom menu
bar).

✦ Click the *settings icon* ⚙ (right corner
of the screen).

  • Select "*Help*" from the "*Settings*"
    page to get to "*Eventbrite Support.*"

▲ Facebook:
https://www.facebook.com

iPhone Facebook App:
https://itunes.apple.com/us/app/facebook/
id284882215?mt=8

Android Facebook App:
https://play.google.com/store/apps/
details?id=com.facebook.katana&hl=en

Facebook Help Center:
https://www.facebook.com/
help/?helpref=facebar_dropdown_help

Facebook Help Center (Mobile App):

✦ Click *"More"* ☰ (bottom menu bar).

✦ Scroll down the page.

✦ Click *"Help and Support."*

✦ A pop-up menu will appear (bottom of the screen).

✦ Select *"Help Center."*

✦ The Facebook Help Center will appear.

✦ Enter the topic you need help with in the main search box.

Other Facebook Help Topics:

Creating and Editing Events:
https://www.facebook.com/help/131325477007622/

Viewing and Responding to Events:
https://www.facebook.com/help/257197944396580/

Sharing and Promoting Events:
https://www.facebook.com/help/656156637816003/

Event Tagging:
https://www.facebook.com/help/264693833649910/

Events Privacy:
https://www.facebook.com/help/216355421820757/

Birthdays And Celebrations:
https://www.facebook.com/
help/422017727841283/

▲ Gravy**:**
https://findgravy.com

iPhone Gravy App:
https://itunes.apple.com/us/app/
gravy-fun-things-to-do-nearby/
id509336320?mt=8

Android Gravy App:
https://play.google.com/store/apps/
details?id=com.timeRAZOR&hl=en

▲ Google+:
https://plus.google.com/

*Switch to Classic Google+ or use Android app
to view "Events"*

Google Hangouts:
http://hangouts.google.com/

Google+ Official Help Page For Events:
https://support.google.com/plus/
answer/2673334?hl=enAndref
topic=2612996

Adding Photos and Videos to Events:
https://support.google.com/plus/
answer/2613195?hl=en

Other Google+ Resources:

How to Create a Google+ Event [Quick Tip]:?
http://blog.hubspot.com/marketing/how-to-create-a-google-plus-event

Ways to Use Google+ Events for Your Business:
http://www.socialmediaexaminer.com/google-plus-events/

▲   Meetup:
https://www.Meetup.com

iPhone Meetup App:
https://itunes.apple.com/us/app/Meetup-groups-near-you-that/id375990038?mt=8

Android Meetup App:
https://play.google.com/store/apps/details?id=com.meetup&hl=en

Meetup Help Center:
http://help.Meetup.com

Meetup Help Center (Mobile App):

✦   Click the *"Profile"* button 🖼 *Profile* (right-hand corner, on the bottom menu bar).

✦   Click *"Settings"* on the profile page.

✦   In settings, click *"Help Center."*

▲ Yelp:
https://www.yelp.com

iPhone Yelp App:
https://itunes.apple.com/us/app/yelp/
id284910350?mt=8

Android Yelp App:
https://play.google.com/store/apps/
details?id=com.yelp.android&hl=en

Yelp Support Center:
http://yelp-support.com

Yelp Support Center (Mobile App):

✦ Click the *"More"* ☰ (bottom menu bar).

✦ The *"More"* menu page will appear.

✦ Scroll down the *"More"* menu page,
and find the section heading that says
"More."

✦ Underneath the *"More"* section
heading, locate and click *"Support."*

✦ The Yelp *"Support Center"* page will
appear.

✦ Type the word *"Events"* in the search
box on the *"Support Center"* page.

✦ Next, click the *"Search Support"* button
to get more help and support with Yelp
events.

Other Yelp Resources:

Yelp Event Terms and Conditions:
http://www.yelp.com/static?p=event_tos

Yelp Elite Members, Additional Terms of Membership:
https://www.yelp.com/tos/elite_en_us_20120425

Find Your Yelp Community Manager:
http://www.yelp.com/elite

Weekly Yelp (Popular Events):
http://www.yelp.com/weekly

Share Your Advice About Yelp Events:
http://bit.ly/YelpEventsAdvice

APPENDIX 3
Networking Resources

Credit Card Readers:

▲ **Square:**
https://squareup.com/reader

▲ **PayPal Here:**
https://paypal.com/here

▲ **Pay Anywhere:**
http://www.payanywhere.com

▲ **Intuit QuickBooks Payments:**
http://payments.intuit.com

▲ **Reviews on Credit Card Readers:**
http://credit-card-processing-review
.toptenreviews.com/mobile-credit-card
-processing/flint-review.html

Personal and Professional Development Resources

- ▲ **Gallup's Clifton Strengthsfinder:**
  https://www.gallupstrengthscenter.com/Purchase/en-US/Index

- ▲ **Myers-Briggs:**
  http://www.mbtionline.com

ABOUT THE AUTHOR

JOHN SPARKS (*@IAmJohnSparks*) is on the 2016 List of Powerful Podcasters, Big Time Bloggers And Social Media Stars Who Can Make You Famous with the Push of a Button (***Push Button Influence, 2016***).

Sparks is also a Top 100 Social Media Power Influencer (***StatSocial, 2015***) and is #13 on the list of the Top 50 Most Valuable Social Media Influencers. His media impact value is $2.1 Million Dollars (***General Sentiment, 2015***).

His first book, "365 Ideas To Go From Good To Great On TWITTER!," soared to #1 on Amazon's Best-Seller list the first weekend it was released on Kindle. The book also received critical praise, especially for its sections on building relationships and community.

Sparks is currently the CEO of his own social media coaching and consulting company called "Online ImageWorks" (@OIWmedia). In addition, he's a veteran newscast producer and an adjunct professor who's taught courses in Advertising at Northwood University and Online Journalism at The University of North Texas.